THE SUBURBAN APARTMENT BOOM

THE SUBURBAN APARTMENT BOOM

CASE STUDY OF A LAND USE PROBLEM

BY MAX NEUTZE

RESOURCES FOR THE FUTURE, INC.
1755 Massachusetts Avenue, N.W., Washington, D.C. 20036

Distributed by THE JOHNS HOPKINS PRESS
Baltimore, Maryland 21218

Resources for the Future is a non-profit corporation for research and education in the development, conservation, and use of natural resources. It was established in 1952 with the co-operation of the Ford Foundation and its activities since then have been financed by grants from the Foundation. Part of the work of Resources for the Future is carried out by its resident staff, part supported by grants to universities and other non-profit organizations. Unless otherwise stated, interpretations and conclusions in RFF publications are those of the authors; the organization takes responsibility for the selection of significant subjects for study, the competence of the researchers, and their freedom of inquiry.

The book is one of RFF's regional and urban studies, which are directed by Harvey S. Perloff. Max Neutze did the research for this study while with RFF as a visiting scholar from The Australian National University. Mr. Neutze is Senior Fellow in Charge, Urban Research Unit, at the University. The figures were drawn by Frank and Clare Ford.

RFF editors: Henry Jarrett, Vera W. Dodds, Nora E. Roots, Sheila M. Ekers

PREFACE

In recent years we have become accustomed, if not resigned, to a sequence of urban crises which stem not only from our numbers but also from our affluence. Rivers become sewers, atmospheres are transformed by chemistry into noxious fogs, landscapes are despoiled. The fact is that our numbers and our affluence have increasingly generated immense pressures on the natural environment which threaten to tax its innate resilience to man-made disturbances. Those elements of the environment which we have thought of as inexhaustible—"pure" air and water, urban space, the radio spectrum, amenity resources—are now relatively in short supply and their stringency grows with each year, with each increment to the population living in cities, with each advance of our prosperity.

To scholars and policy makers alike, these changes in the quality of the urban environment have disclosed the inadequacy of the conventional theories and concepts to predict the future states of degradation of the environment or to suggest feasible social strategies to deal with them. Our present conceptual equipment comes from an earlier age in response to other kinds of situations and policy issues; it has at best a limited usefulness in helping us to cope with the great problems of our own age. Fresh concepts and theories reflecting these newly crucial relationships between the intense life of the city and its natural setting will need to be formulated. Thus, it is becoming obvious to us now that every city is sensitively articulated with a resource base—its physical environment. Shifts in function and in sources of resource value are pronounced enough to warrant our speaking of "new resources" in an urban, "post-industrial" age. Urban land, for example, might best be viewed as *urban space,* with value derived in large part from access characteristics—access to the center, to the transportation network, and to all other points in the urban plane—as well as from its physical properties and amenity characteristics. Transformation in modes of thought to match transformation of the environment is necessary if policy instruments are to be designed capable of dealing with environmental-quality issues.

Resources for the Future has responded to this challenge by sponsoring a series of studies on the resource base in the urban environment.

The present volume in this series, by Max Neutze, was based on research carried out by the author during a year spent with RFF as a visiting scholar. Mr. Neutze is Senior Fellow in Charge, Urban Research Unit, at The Australian National University.

The urban transformation that concerns Neutze here is the marked increase in construction of apartment residences in the suburbs and, more remarkably, to a considerable extent in the suburban fringes. A development that is unexpected offers a special opportunity to discover where derived theory is inadequate; "surprises" in social science thus provide a special laboratory-like situation.

Neutze traces through in some detail the extent and character of suburban apartment construction and considers the multitude of factors behind this interesting change by means of an in-depth study of the Washington metropolitan region and through a comparison of forty-one large U.S. metropolitan areas. Carefully he develops the logic behind what has been taking place, showing why the suburban apartment boom can best be understood as the latest phase of suburbanization, influenced by demographic factors (there is a whole generation of young persons reared in the suburbs who are choosing to start married life there), suburban subcenter and highway development, and the impact of established national and local policies, including tax and zoning policies.

The latter he finds particularly worthy of attention. The general public, he notes, often fails to grasp how its environment is being influenced by certain policies pushed by individuals and groups with narrow special interests; it is not necessarily getting what it thinks it is bargaining for. He demonstrates this by setting up a policy "model" suggesting what an optimum role for local government in the urban land market might be, and then contrasts actual policy with such optimal policy. While readers may not fully agree with his policy conclusions, they will be stimulated to new insights by his provocative formulation.

Harvey S. Perloff
Director, Regional and Urban Studies
August 1968
Resources for the Future, Inc.

ACKNOWLEDGMENTS

This study was largely completed during a year at Resources for the Future while I was on study leave from The Australian National University. More, perhaps, than most, it reflects the insight gained in talking to government officials and private developers involved in urban development. Harvey S. Perloff, of Resources for the Future, first suggested the study and gave invaluable assistance during the year, as did Lowdon Wingo, Jr. and Marion Clawson, also of RFF. Lewis Elston of the Maryland National Capital Park and Planning Commission introduced me to the zoning system in Montgomery County and helped me to understand it. Robert M. Steinberg assisted with the computer calculations. The analysis is much more logical and coherent as a result of very extensive comments made by Irving Hoch of RFF on an earlier draft. The conclusions are, of course, entirely my own and those who have given me help bear no responsibility for them.

Max Neutze

CONTENTS

1. Introduction 1
   Types of Land Use 3
   The Scale of Development 5
   Recent Trends in Apartment Building 8
      The United States 8
      Census tracts of the Washington SMSA 9
      Montgomery County, Maryland 12

2. Some Reasons for the Apartment Boom 21
   Demographic factors 22
      Age composition of the population 22
      Household formation 23
   Mobility and the House Owner as Speculator 27
   Relative Building Costs 29
   Income Tax Provisions 31
   Changing Tastes 34

3. Apartments in the Suburbs 37
   Migrations to the Suburbs 37
   The Slow Rate of Redevelopment in Central Areas 40
   Racial Discrimination 41
   Local Government Revenue and Expenditure 42
   Land Speculation and Zoning Policies 44

4. Apartments on the Suburban Fringe 51
   Urban Expressways and Market Differentiation 52
   Location of Employment 53
   Retirement Communities 54
   Utility Policy 55
   Zoning 55
   Speculation 58
   Washington SMSA Census Tracts 60
   The Experience of Montgomery and Fairfax Counties . . . 69
   High-Rise Building on the Suburban Fringe 80

5. Comparisons between Metropolitan Areas 86
   The Data 86
   The Building Cycle Hypothesis 90
   The Extent of the Apartment Boom 93
      Variations in the proportion of apartments,
         1960–65 94
      Variations in the relative increase in the proportion of
         apartments after 1960 96
   The Suburban Apartment Boom 99
      Variations in the proportion of apartments in
         the suburbs 101
      Variations in the relative increase of suburban
         apartments 103
      Variations in the relative increase of the proportion of
         SMSA apartments in the suburbs 104

6. Land Use Decisions and Imperfections in the Land Market . . 105
   The Development-Redevelopment Decision 105
   Market Imperfections and Their Effects 109
      Land speculation 109
      Imperfections of the capital market 113
      External effects of land use decisions 118
      Monopoly and imperfect competition 120
      Frictions in the market 121

**7. An Optimal Role for Government in the
Urban Land Market** 123
   Operations of the Government through the Price System . . 123
      Forecasting and control 127
   A Planning Solution to the Land Use Problem 134

8. The Effects of Non-Optimal Public Policy 138
   Charges for Utility Investment 138
   User Charges 141
   Property Taxes 144
   Externalities 148
   Co-ordination and Forecasting 153
   Intrametropolitan Area Competition 154
   Federal Government Taxes 157
   Federal Credit 163
   Conclusions 164

9. Summary 165
   Private and Public Decisions in the Urban Land Market . . . 165
   The Suburban Apartment Boom 167
   Some Gaps That Should Be Closed 169

LIST OF TABLES

1. Total and one-family non-farm housing unit starts in the
   United States, 1940–1965 9

2. Apartments as a percentage of housing units in areas within
   the Washington SMSA 11

3. Location of major types of housing units within the
   Washington SMSA, 1960 and 1966 12

4. Changes in the distribution of apartment units within
   Montgomery County 14

5. Trends in apartment size: suburban Washington 24

6. Schoolchildren per 100 apartment units: Montgomery
   County 26

7. Changes in the capacity of apartment-zoned land:
   Montgomery County, 1959–1966 46

8. Frequency of local employment 54

9. Census tracts: Washington SMSA changes with distance
   from the center 63

10. Building and rezoning by district: Montgomery County . . . 68

11. District comparisons: Montgomery County 76

12. Time trends in apartment characteristics: Montgomery and
    Fairfax counties 77

13. Density by date and district: Montgomery County 78

14. Significance of apartments in forty-one SMSA's 88

15. Correlation between percentage of apartments and total
    number of permits issued in forty-one SMSA's 92

16. The changing role of the suburbs in the housing market . . . 100

17. The value of tax concessions to apartment and house owners . 159

18. Marginal tax rates required to equalize present value of concessions of apartment owners with those of house owners . . 160

LIST OF FIGURES

1. Lower Montgomery County showing district boundaries and apartments, June 1966 15

2. Boeckh indexes of dwelling unit costs 29

3. Estimated construction costs of non-farm starts 30

4. Apartments as a percentage of total housing by rings: Washington SMSA 65

5. Optimal building height 81

6. Effect of height premium on optimal height 83

7. Effect of land price on optimal height 84

8. The apartment building cycle in selected SMSA's, 1960–1965 . 91

THE SUBURBAN APARTMENT BOOM

chapter 1

INTRODUCTION

In the middle 1950's, housing market analysts were concerned with the reasons for the demise of the apartment as a form of accommodation.[1] A satisfactory explanation appeared to be to the effect that, as people become richer, their demand for living space increases and can best be satisfied by a single-family house on its own plot in the suburbs. By 1965 the wheel had turned a full circle and single-family housing was in the doldrums while apartments comprised a high proportion of all dwelling units being constructed.

There have been booms in apartment construction before but this one appears to be unusual in a number of respects. The apartments are much less concentrated in central city areas than previously. Again, of course, apartments in the suburbs are no new phenomenon. Garden apartments were constructed in the suburbs at least as long ago as the 1920's. The unusual thing about the boom is its magnitude rather than its nature. A higher proportion of apartments is being built in the suburbs—and further out in the suburbs—than in central areas, and there has been a much more rapid growth in apartment than in single-family house building in the suburbs. There are also more high-density apartments in suburban areas than previously. The most spectacular, though not the most typical, manifestation of the boom is the high-rise apartment on the suburban fringe.

The objective of this monograph is to shed some light on two related questions. First, what is occurring and why? Why do apartment builders, who can afford to pay for land that is much more accessible to the city center, choose instead to locate in the suburbs? Why has the boom in suburban apartment construction occurred and what kinds of apartments are being built? Second, is the building of suburban apartments—as compared with suburban homes on the one hand, or central area apartments on the other—being unduly encouraged by market imperfections or by public policy? The first question is positive and asks for reasons, the second is normative and asks for evaluation.

In this monograph an attempt is made to answer these questions First, possible answers are examined in the light of the recent experi-

1. A good example is Louis Winnick, *Rental Housing: Opportunities for Private Investment* (McGraw-Hill, 1958). Winnick did predict an upturn, though a more modest one, and later than it actually occurred.

ence of the Washington metropolitan area, and Montgomery County in particular. Next, events on a national level are considered and the experiences of forty-one large metropolitan areas are compared. Some theoretical models relevant to land use decisions are then developed and used to answer the second question, evaluating the important features of the boom. The Washington Standard Metropolitan Statistical Area (SMSA) and Montgomery County are not typical of other parts of the country, but those who are acquainted with other specific areas can make use of that information which is applicable and reject that which is peculiar to this area. The analysis leaves many questions unanswered. My objective is to provide a framework for the analysis of the two questions and to look at some parts of the framework in more detail. Perhaps the questions asked will be of more value than the answers provided.

The latter part of this chapter introduces the study, first with a dis cussion of types of land use—of apartments in particular—and then with an overview of developments in the housing situation in the Washington metropolitan area and in the nation. It also introduces the data that will be used in analyzing the changes that have taken place in the local housing stock since 1960. In the next three chapters, the nature of and the reasons for the apartment boom are examined, using data for the Washington SMSA and Montgomery County to see whether some of the explanations commonly advanced are supported by the facts in these areas. Although I believe that most of the possible reasons for the boom are mentioned in these chapters, only some of them are tested as hypotheses and my only evidence of the importance of some is the opinion of other research workers in this field and the views of actual operators in the urban land market. In Chapter 5, some hypotheses about the nature of the suburban apartment boom are tested by comparing the experience of forty-one large SMSA's during the period 1960–65.

In Chapter 6, a theoretical model of land use determination in urban areas is developed. Although some good work has been done on long-run models which show the form the urban area would be expected to take if everything was in equilibrium, the short run has been neglected. Chapter 6 attempts to fill part of this gap and to supplement, rather than supplant, the long-run model as a framework for analysis. It also begins the evaluation of the boom with an examination of the effects of the imperfections of the urban land market and of the way in which they could be expected to influence the volume of suburban apartment building. The chapter is largely theoretical since information in this area is difficult to collect. Chapter 7 is also theoretical and continues the process of evaluation by examining the role that governments should play in the urban land market, both as providers of public goods and services (and therefore users of land) and as planners and controllers of private land use decisions. I feel that a better basic understanding of the role governments should play is essential if planning is to be more effective in shaping urban areas in ways that maximize community welfare, however that may be defined. But, for the purposes of this monograph, Chapter 7 provides a standard against which actual policy can be assessed. Chapter 8 compares the policies which governments (and the Montgomery County government in particular) have been using, with the optimum policy prescription, and looks at the effects of non-optimal policy prescription on the volume and location of apartment construction. Chapter 9 provides a brief summary and review, and some suggestions for further fruitful research.

Types of Land Use

One way to classify land uses is by the price users of the land can afford to pay. This kind of classification is fairly broadly related to a number of other features, some of which have been recognized in zoning laws.

Extent of Area Used. At any given level, the users requiring the greatest quantity of land per unit of output can generally afford to pay least for it. For the country as a whole, agriculture and forestry cover the greatest area and users in these spheres cannot afford to pay rents as high as those paid by transport networks, most recreational facilities, and urban land users. Within an urban area, residences take up the greatest area and land used for this purpose is the least valuable. Industrial and commercial users occupy much smaller areas and are able to pay much more for the land they use.

Sensitivity of Profits to the Use of Surrounding Land. Those land users who can pay high rents for a small area of land have to face the possibility that their competitors may find better locations relative to surrounding land uses. Consequently, given the basic technical sensitivity of a particular land use to the use of other land in the neighborhood, the smaller the area of land used, the more sensitive its profits will be to surrounding land uses. This can apply to apartments and to single-family housing. Apartments occupy a much smaller proportion of the land in most cities than do single-family houses and, partly as a consequence, are more sensitive to the use of land nearby.

Uncertainty. Because profits are more sensitive to the use of land in surrounding areas, when much of the nearby land is not committed to a specific use, there is rather more uncertainty in building apartments, a shopping center, or an industrial park than in building houses.

Timing. One way in which this uncertainty can be kept to a minimum is by postponing development until the nature of the surrounding development is known. As a consequence, the kind of development mainly found at the edge of the urban fringe is single-family housing. Apartments and commercial and industrial land uses follow, sometimes making use of land which has been withheld from single-family housing development by speculation (passive or active).

"Higher Uses." American zoning law recognizes some kind of ranking of land uses from higher to lower. Commercial and industrial uses are at the lower and single-family residential uses at the higher end. The ranking is clearly related to the rents that can be paid but there is also an implicit judgment about the direction of externalities. A so-called higher use may occupy land which is zoned for a lower use, but not vice versa. The implication, if zoning is a means of preventing undesirable effects of externalities on land use, seems to be that lower land uses have undesirable external effects on higher land uses but that the reverse is not true. Indeed, it has been stated that industries tend to "blight" a residential area but that residences do not harmfully affect an industrial area.

This seems to contradict the ranking of land uses according to their sensitivity to externalities. But the breadth of choice of location enters into the "high-lower" use ranking in almost the opposite way that it does into my sensitivity ranking. Whereas a wide choice of location increases the sensitivity of those using land for such purposes to competition from others who are more favorably located, it also gives less excuse for the intrusion of the lower uses into areas which they would adversely affect. It is consistent to say that apartments have an adverse effect on single-family housing rather than vice versa, and that profits from apartments are more susceptible than those from houses to the use of surrounding land.

Traditionally, when the most favorable location for almost any land use in a city was the center, uses which could justify users paying the highest rents were located nearest the center, surrounded by those which could justify the next highest rents, and so on, producing a pattern of location and rents not unlike von Thünen's rings in the theory of agricultural location. Even when the automobile made city centers congested, permitted the suburban explosion, and made shopping centers and garden apartments optimal suburban land uses, these latter uses still appeared mainly as a second wave of urban development, occupying land which had been bypassed for some reason, or sometimes replacing some low-density buildings. Apartments and shopping centers tended to be clustered close together in the more accessible parts of the suburban areas and to be close to those centers of employment which had moved out of the city center.

Recently, increasing numbers of apartments have been appearing at the fringe of urban development. This poses a question: Are apartments becoming so important that they are taking over the role of single-family housing in urban development, or is the relationship breaking down between extent of area used, choice of location, sensitivity to surrounding land use, and timing of development? In the following chapters a number of reasons for this phenomenon are examined, but, for the most part, it seems that it does not represent a breakdown of the previous orders of development. Even on the outskirts of cities like Washington, single-family housing is still by far the most extensive use of land. Although more apartments than single-family houses have recently been built in some suburban areas, because of the differences in density they occupy a far smaller area of new land.

Apartments are certainly not being scattered indiscriminately, either around the periphery of the built-up areas or in the areas "ripe for re-development." Developers are very sensitive to variations in accessibility to good highways, shopping centers, recreation, and open space on the urban fringe. Near the city centers they give considerable weight to a prestigious address, nearness to employment centers, good shops and cultural amenities, and to the character of the neighborhood. One feature of the urban land market that the apartment boom may have accentuated is its spatial differentiation. The accessibility and character of an area can change in a few blocks in the central area and in less than a mile in the suburbs. Accessibility is not necessarily measured in distance from employment, shopping, etc., as such, but more frequently in distance from a good highway or good public transport.

The Scale of Development

One feature of apartment development on the urban fringe is the size of individual undertakings. Developments numbering hundreds of apartments are common and the smaller developments tend to cluster either close to the larger ones or close to some shopping or employment center. The large development can internalize many of the externalities which are a source of uncertainty to the smaller development. It can provide its own recreational facilities and often supplies enough consumer demand to ensure the establishment of a shopping center nearby if this is desired. For the large-scale developer there are two great advantages in building on the outskirts rather than in an established area. One is that it is easier and cheaper to assemble a large contiguous site; the other is that land, even the choicest, is much cheaper. But a large-scale development itself adds value to the land, and this capital gain is part of the return. It would generally be smaller in an established area.

Developers choosing this alternative are still in the minority for, offsetting the advantages, are both the likelihood of higher vacancy rates and the costs of providing better facilities to entice people to live further from the city center, and, in most cases, from their places of work. Many large-scale developments exist in the suburban centers and in the city centers themselves. The apartment in the green fields is partly catering to a special taste—a taste that may put more weight on the closeness of recreation, open spaces, and special cultural facilities, and give a negative weight to maintaining the grounds and structure of a house. Apartments catering to this or similar tastes are not necessarily less certain ventures than their more central competitors, except in the sense that they are competing for a market that is probably narrower.

In fact, each type of fringe apartment development has some way of hedging against the uncertainty that the simple model would lead us to expect it to encounter. It either depends on nearby land uses, such as freeways and golf courses, which are already present; or on other apartment developments; or it is large enough to be able to internalize many of the land use decisions which are external to the smaller development. Thus, apartment builders are still able to choose the most suitable land for their purposes, even though they sometimes make the choice at a relatively early stage in the process of urbanization, look for different features than previously, and are more independent as the size of developments becomes larger. The location of large developments tends to determine, rather than being determined by, the shape of growth.

Many of the same factors apply to redevelopment areas, though they seem to be more in accord with the classical model. Redevelopers who operate on a large scale are the only ones who can really be venturesome and move into slum areas any distance from existing redevelopment. These areas will then attract some smaller redevelopments which are not themselves large enough to alter the character of their neighborhood, and thus mostly occur in the vicinity of existing redevelopments. As a result, redevelopment tends to creep along the main thoroughfares and only very slowly spreads into their hinterlands. This is possibly because the existing buildings remain as the most extensive land use in such areas and will continue to remain so as long as income distribution, housing costs, and discrimination combine to produce very large demands for that type of accommodation. A good deal of stress has been placed on the advantages of the large-scale development that can internalize many of the external effects on the value of land. Also, although there may not be any formal market through which the developer can influence other landowners and developers, he often seems to find ways of influencing the use of surrounding land. Increases in land value are very largely a function of changes in the use of other land in the neighborhood and the provision of public facilities. Even if there is no planning to ensure that shopping centers and apartments are built near one another, adjacent landowners can often mutually benefit from getting together. An apartment builder who does not wish to extend his operations may buy adjacent land and sell it on favorable terms for a shopping center, give it to a non-profit swimming club, pay for a golf club house nearby, or provide street access for a complementary development.

There have been many instances in which a private developer has made the same kinds of offers to local government, or has been required to provide some facilities in return for the privilege of higher-density zoning. But in many cases the terms have been mutually beneficial. Land for street widening is certainly the most common requirement and the residents of an apartment development benefit from wider streets. If a developer gives, or sells cheaply, land for a school, he can advertise a convenient school for the children of his tenants.

In both cases, speculative profits are an incentive for co-ordination of land use development. It will be profitable for the individual developer to spend any amount up to the resultant increase in the value of his land in order to induce changes in the use of other land which increase the value of his own. Although this is an imperfect process and the highest profits are sometimes made by those who wait and hope for favorable developments without spending anything, it does suggest that the process of land use co-ordination occurs to some extent, even in the absence of planning. In later chapters it will be shown that the process can occur in a similar way if an existing plan is found by developers to be manipulable. In Chapter 7 it is suggested that planning would be more efficient if it either used and worked through the speculative incentive for private co-ordination, or else explicitly took over this role for itself.

Land speculation can be defined as the influence on land use of expected future increases in its value, and speculative land uses as those which depend heavily on such increases. For example, apartments are more speculative than single-family housing: first, because the relatively large size of the typical undertaking allows a good deal of internalization of externalities; second, because they have a greater dependence on uses of other land in the neighborhood, as discussed above; and third, because the developer can economically hold apartments after they are built and rent them while their value continues to increase. In this way the increases in land value after, as well as before, actual development can be captured by the developer.

Recent Trends in Apartment Building

The United States. Table 1 shows the volume of non-farm housing starts for the whole country for each year from 1940 to 1965, and the percentage of one-family in total starts. From the end of World War II until 1960, single-family houses never accounted for less than 77 per cent of the total; in most years the percentage was over 80, and very frequently it was in the high 80's. The only dip occurred in 1949 when for a short period the federal government provided so liberal a credit for building apartments that the developer had almost zero equity in the project. But by 1960 there was some evidence of a trend, or at least a long-term cyclical shift, away from single-family houses. The total volume of single-family housing has not fallen very much since then but there has been a marked increase in apartment building.

In Table 1 housing units are divided into only two categories. [For some purposes apartments will later be defined more restrictively in order to exclude duplexes (two-unit structures).] During the 1960's all intermediate types of structures, which may be thought of as containing two to four housing units, have declined as a proportion of starts. What may be considered as apartments proper (5 or more units) have comprised around one-third of the starts in each of the years 1963 to 1965. The latest information available at the time of writing showed that the credit restrictions of 1966 were having little effect on the proportions of one-family units among housing starts although building permit figures suggest that the credit shortage was tending to reduce the volume of multiple-family housing. The intermediate types of structures were suffering very much, probably because the recession hit hardest in California where this type of housing is most popular.

The boom in single-family housing during the 1950's was strong enough to have a marked effect on the composition of the total housing stock. The 1950 Census showed that 63.9 per cent of the country's housing units were single-family detached structures; by 1960, this had risen to 70.0 per cent. During this period, attached single-unit and two-to-four-unit structures fell from 25.0 per cent to 19.3 per cent of the

Table 1. Total and One-Family Non-Farm Housing Unit Starts in the United States, 1940–1965

Year	One-family units	Two- or more-family units	Total	Per cent one-family units
	(. . . . . 1,000 . . . .)			
1940	486	117	603	76.12%
1941	604	102	706	85.47
1942	293	63	356	82.25
1943	144	47	191	75.18
1944	118	24	142	83.00
1945	185	24	209	88.20
1946	590	81	671	87.99
1947	740	109	849	87.18
1948	767	165	932	82.29
1949	794	231	1,025	77.49
1950	1,154	242	1,396	82.67
1951	900	191	1,091	82.48
1952	943	184	1,127	83.63
1953	938	166	1,104	84.96
1954	1,078	142	1,220	88.32
1955	1,194	135	1,329	89.88
1956	990	128	1,118	88.52
1957	873	169	1,042	83.76
1958	975	224	1,209	80.63
1959	1,095	284	1,379	79.41
New series[a]				
1959	1,229	302	1,531	80.24
1960	987	287	1,274	77.44
1961	961	376	1,337	71.88
1962	973	496	1,469	66.24
1963	994	619	1,613	61.62
1964	946	618	1,564	60.49
1965	941	579	1,520	61.91

[a] The new series includes figures from a substantially larger number of reporting local authorities.

Sources: 1940–60: U.S. Department of Housing and Urban Development, *Housing Statistics,* Historical Supplement (October 1961), p. 5. 1961–65: *Housing Statistics,* Annual Data (May 1966), Table A–3.

total, and structures with five or more units fell from 11.0 per cent to 10.7 per cent. Table 1 highlights one of the problems encountered by this study—because the apartment boom occurred mainly after 1960, the census figures for that year are of little value in analyzing it. However, they do provide a base from which the analysis can start.

Census tracts of the Washington SMSA. Each of the large local governments in the Washington metropolitan area keeps estimates of the volume of house building by census tract. Since the main objective is to keep an up-to-date estimate of population changes by tract, they try to count the housing units at the time they are occupied, or at least become ready for occupation. In some cases this is done by assuming that a house is occupied some fixed period after the permit is issued and checking on any permits that lapse or are withdrawn. In other cases the records are taken from Assessors' offices, either when the buildings come on to the rolls or when a certificate of occupancy is issued. As indicators of the gross level of building activity, these statistics appear to be quite reliable.

Demolitions and changes in use are recorded in a rather less systematic way in most jurisdictions, and this makes it rather difficult to link the figures to those from the 1960 Census. One tract near the center of Washington showed five housing units in 1960, but in the following five years no less than one hundred and fifty were demolished. Although they were housing-type structures, most of them had been converted to other uses or had been vacated before 1960. In the outlying areas demolitions are relatively unimportant—in Montgomery County there were 106 in 1965. In the inner areas they are much more important. In all cases an attempt was made to get as close as possible to a figure for net change in the number of one- and two-family units, and of three-or-more-family units.[2]

A small number of tracts which are dominated by institutions were eliminated from the analysis. The Bureau of the Census, *1960 Census of Population and Housing,* PHC (1), figures were used to provide a base from which to operate. They were also used for estimates, at that date, of median family income, proportion of the 1960 housing stock more than twenty years old at that date, distance of the tract from the Federal Triangle (the main center of federal employment), and the proportion of the work force using public transport for the journey to work.

Although the District of Columbia is the central city of the SMSA, the county of Arlington and the city of Alexandria in Virginia are in many respects similar to it. They are intermediate between central areas and the fully suburban counties which surround them. Table 2 shows the percentage of apartments (defined as units in structures with three or more units) in the major areas within the SMSA in 1960 and the percent-

---

2. Alexandria and Fairfax publish net changes only. Prince Georges and Montgomery counties' data completely omit demolitions. Arlington and the District of Columbia record gross and net changes, but in the District the figures for "numbers of units razed" do not distinguish between houses and apartments, and some apartment buildings that have been razed are counted as one unit. All units razed in the District are assumed, in my estimates, to be single-family houses, whether attached or detached.

Table 2. Apartments as a Percentage of Housing Units in Areas Within the Washington SMSA[a]

Area	1/4/60 Census	Housing unit permits issued						Estimated % in stock[b] 1/1/66
		1960	1961	1962	1963	1964	1965	
Washington, D.C.	54.0%	88.8%	87.2%	93.1%	96.1%	94.5%	96.0%	58.5%
Arlington County	47.4	76.0	70.8	89.4	83.4	92.4	89.2	53.2
Alexandria	40.5	62.8	87.3	95.5	94.6	93.0	96.9	54.3
Prince Georges County	24.5	46.8	51.9	60.5	75.8	58.3	73.2	37.8
Montgomery County	17.0	41.8	39.3	50.1	55.2	42.8	67.4	23.2
Fairfax County	9.3	7.4	34.0	48.6	43.7	53.2	50.5	19.4

[a] Apartments are units in structures containing three or more units.
[b] Sources of stock change data are discussed in the text.
Sources: U.S. Bureau of the Census, *1960 Census of Population and Housing,* Series PHC (1), Census Tracts (Washington, 1960); U.S. Bureau of the Census, *Construction Reports* (C40), (Annual; Washington, 1960–65).

age among permits issued yearly from 1960 to 1965. Apart from Fairfax County, which lagged a little in getting on the bandwagon, the trend towards apartments has been consistent and shows no signs of abating or of the cyclical downturn observed in many SMSA's. The building of single-family houses has almost ceased in the inner areas. In both Montgomery and Prince Georges counties, more permits were issued for apartment units in the three years from 1963 to 1965 than were in existence in 1960; in Fairfax County, twice as many were issued. The changing climate for apartments since 1960 can be illustrated from a report published by the Maryland National Capital Park and Planning Commission (MNCPPC) in that year which predicted that the number of apartment units in Montgomery County would rise from 12,800 in 1958 to 23,800 in 1980, and in Prince Georges County from 31,150 to 43,800 in this period.[3] On January 1, 1966, 30,147 apartment units were on the Assessor's rolls in Montgomery County and 61,376 in Prince Georges County.

The figures in Table 2 (except in the last column) indicate gross building activity. Although some permits lapse, under normal circumstances the number is small, since the cost of a permit is not negligible. To find the net change in housing units, demolitions must be subtracted. Table 3 shows the numbers of housing units of each type in 1960 and an estimate of the numbers on January 1, 1966. It is necessarily inaccurate because of conversions, because demolitions are underestimated in some

3. Maryland National Capital Park and Planning Commission, A *Preliminary Master Plan of Residential Land Use* (Silver Spring and Riverdale, Md., July 1960), p. 63.

areas, and because conversions from single-family to multiple-family use are not taken into account. The table also shows that outer areas have very markedly increased their share in the SMSA apartment market. This change has been much more marked than the increase in the outer-area share of the single-family house market—an increase that would be expected to result from traditional metropolitan expansion.

Table 3. Location of Major Types of Housing Units within the Washington SMSA, 1960 and 1966

	1960				January 1, 1966[a]			
	Number of units		Per cent of SMSA		Number of units		Per cent of SMSA	
Area	1 + 2 family	3 + family	1 + 2 family	3 + family	1 + 2 family	3 + family	1 + 2 family	3 + family
Washington, D.C.	120,865	141,774	31.0%	62.1%	117,156	165,070	26.0%	49.4%
Arlington County	29,983	26,963	7.7	11.8	31,089	35,297	6.9	10.6
Alexandria	17,711	12,043	4.5	5.3	18,367	21,865	4.1	6.5
Prince Georges County	75,709	24,398	19.3	10.7	100,845	61,376	22.4	18.4
Montgomery County	80,655	16,476	20.7	7.2	99,714	30,147	22.1	9.0
Fairfax County	65,404	6,671	16.8	2.9	83,841	20,205	18.6	6.1

a Estimated.
Source: U.S. Bureau of the Census, 1960 Census of Population and Housing, PHC (1). Figures on net additions to housing stock prepared by planning departments and commissions.

Montgomery County, Maryland. North of the District of Columbia, Montgomery County forms the northern section of the part of the Washington SMSA that lies in Maryland. As in many suburban areas, metropolitan development has already engulfed, or is in the process of engulfing, towns and villages which once existed as separate settlements. While some—such as Silver Spring, just outside the District— have been surrounded and become suburban centers, others further out—such as Rockville, the county seat, and Gaithersburg—have not yet been immersed. Each of the two latter centers has some political autonomy from the county, and each makes its own zoning decisions. Rockville, in particular, is a significant employment center. For a part of the work force, access to these centers, or to employment centers elsewhere in the county, is more important than access to downtown Washington.

From records in the offices of the County Assessor and the Building Inspector, a list was made of all apartments first placed on the Assessor's rolls between January 1960 and June 1966, and of building permits that had been issued at that date for apartment buildings not yet on the Assessor's rolls. The sizes of units (number of bedrooms) in some of the buildings were obtained from building permits and apartment shoppers' guides. The numbers of elementary, junior high school, and senior high school students in certain apartment buildings were obtained from the County School Board records, which generally included only buildings which yielded a significant number of school children. In both cases the sample of apartments for which information was available had a preponderance of larger buildings.

In the analysis of the figures some use has been made of assessed land value, but this does not give a very accurate reflection of current market value since reassessment of existing projects occurs only at intervals of several years. Some of the assessments are, therefore, out of date, especially in areas of rapid change. When apartments are being built, land values are not reassessed up to the level appropriate for apartment land until the building is at least partly occupied. As a consequence, land values for plots where permits are outstanding are of little value in the present analysis. Normally, building permit figures are a good indicator of the number of units that will be built within the next year or so, although the proportion of large projects may be over-estimated because of their longer gestation period. In Montgomery County, the zoning ordinance was changed to restrict the building of apartments in areas zoned for commercial uses, and the last date for permit applications on the old basis was April 25, 1966. A large number of applications were made in the first months of 1966 to beat this deadline. If these were all completed there would almost certainly be over-building. A more realistic assessment of the market prospects, combined with a shortage of credit, has caused a considerable slowdown in the rate of starts. In fact, a number of the permit applications had not, late in 1966, been processed. The data in this study take into account only those permits that were issued. Some apartments probably will not be built, and others will not be built until credit becomes easier, although quite a number are actually under construction. However, the permit application figures are distorted and some of the analyses will omit them.

Although some analyses use the continuous variable "distance from the District boundary," as a location indicator, it is occasionally convenient to express the results by distinguishing different districts within the urban part of Montgomery County. Table 4 and Figure 1 provide a summary of apartment building within the county during the 1960's and show the location of the outstanding apartment building permits, excluding the Gaithersburg area (electoral district 9), north of Rockville.

Table 4. Changes in the Distribution of Apartment Units within Montgomery County

(Dwelling units)

Date built	Silver Spring—Takoma Park	Bethesda—Chevy Chase	Wheaton—Kensington	Grosvenor—Twinbrook	Potomac	Wheaton—Outer	Coles-ville	Rock-ville	Gaithers-burg	Total
Before 1960	10,079	3,490	41	280	0	0	747	890	341	15,868
1960	2,209	298	0	0	0	0	0	182	27	2,716
1961	1,071	38	484	170	0	0	0	445	62	2,270
1962	337	529	328	0	317	289	0	531	241	2,572
1963	810	85	33	215	59	217	0	401	170	1,990
1964	349	237	227	623	108	0	534	303	296	2,677
1965	380	77	0	984	0	268	576	0	132	2,417
1966[a]	366	76	182	1,020	0	48	415	202	429	2,738
Permits outstanding	4,236	6,202	1,312	2,875	0	1,408	1,565	322	235	18,155
Total	19,837	11,032	2,607	6,167	484	2,230	3,837	3,276	1,933	51,403

[a] First six months only.

Sources: Before 1960: Lusk Montgomery County Apartment Directory (Washington, D.C.: Rufus S. Lusk and Sons, 1963); Maryland National Capital Park and Planning Commission, Residential Land Use (July 1960). Since 1960: Assessor's rolls and building permits.

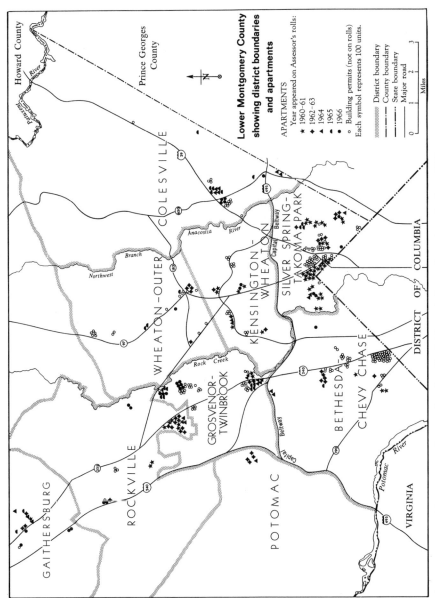

Figure 1. Lower Montgomery County showing district boundaries and apartments, June 1966

Since the districts have been chosen to reflect some of the important qualitative differences, they can be described by the features which might loom largest in the decisions of apartment developers. *Bethesda–Chevy Chase* (between Rock Creek and the Beltway) is a very high-income part of the county adjacent to the District boundary. It was largely developed for urban purposes in 1960. Some single-family house building has taken place in the area during the 1960's, mainly in the parts that are most distant from the District. The commercial center is only moderately strong and, in 1960, included no very high-density developments. However, in the northern part, the National Institutes of Health and the Naval Medical Center provide a very substantial volume of local employment.

Silver Spring–Takoma Park (between Rock Creek, Northwest Branch, and the Beltway) is the other part of the county which borders the District. It also was fully developed in 1960. However, income levels are, for the most part, lower and the standard of the older single-family houses is correspondingly lower. There are a number of row houses, especially in Takoma Park. The Silver Spring commercial center is probably the strongest in the whole SMSA outside downtown Washington. It contains a large shopping area and is also an important office center. The circumferential Beltway (Interstate Route 495) forms an appropriate boundary between these two inner areas and the outer areas.

The *Kensington–Wheaton* area (between Rock Creek, Northwest Branch, the Beltway, and a line from Wheaton Regional Park to Rock Creek Pallisades School) is, in some respects, intermediate between inner and outer areas. Although developed much more recently than most parts of the two inner areas, in 1960 it was substantially urbanized and was more fully developed than any of the contiguous suburban areas outside the Beltway. However, it was much younger, and did not have as much commercial development as the inner areas. Little single-family house building has taken place within the area during the 1960's. Income levels are about average for the county; i.e., high both for the SMSA and for the whole country.

The area extending north from Wheaton is called *Wheaton–Outer*. Although it includes a good deal of land which is still not occupied by urban uses, it did have a large finger of development between Georgia Avenue and Rock Creek in 1960. Like other fringe areas it has its share of large lot single-family housing. However, in 1960 it had a greater volume of contiguous small lot (mostly five to seven to the acre) one-family housing than the other major fringe areas—Colesville, Potomac, or Grosvenor–Twinbrook—despite the fact that it is somewhat farther from the downtown area.

Colesville comprises the area between Northwest Branch and the Prince Georges County line. Although largely undeveloped in 1960, there was a small area in the corner close to Takoma Park which was quite fully developed and even contained a large block of garden apartments. *Potomac* (Election District 10) contained a few small villages in 1960 and a good deal of large lot development. Although it is relatively close to the District, it has lagged considerably in full suburbanization. This appears to have been no accident, but the result of the policy of a well-organized group of residents and landowners in the area. They have provided strong political opposition to rezoning proposals, and appear to have exerted pressure on local landowners not to build apartments or to sell to apartment builders.

The *Grosvenor–Twinbrook* area is difficult to define. It extends from Rock Creek to U.S. Route 70S and from the Beltway to the Rockville corporate limits. In 1960 it had relatively little development. There were some areas of single-family housing, a good deal of strip development along Rockville Pike, and the first of the high income Parkside garden apartments in the south. There has been an intensification of the strip development, broadening in some places into wholesaling and a light industrial park. Substantial areas are still vacant.

Gaithersburg (the whole of Election District 9—not shown in Figure 1) is far enough away from the District that, until recently, it could be regarded as a separate housing market. With the opening of Route 70S it became more accessible. However, most of the features of apartments built there during the 1960's are what would be expected in a town of its size (population 9,000 in 1960 and 13,000 in 1966).

Rockville (the corporate city plus most of Census Tract 12B) is in a much more mixed situation. It was a separate entity before there was very much suburban development in Montgomery County. It is the county seat and has a good deal of local employment. However, there was a considerable amount of undeveloped land within the corporate limits in 1960 and the subsequent development of this land has been oriented more to metropolitan Washington than to Rockville city. Whereas the change in orientation of the housing market in Gaithersburg may be just occurring now, it probably occurred in Rockville around or before 1960. The Rockville corporate limits also extended beyond the 1960 boundary of urban development to a much greater extent than did the limits of Gaithersburg. In contrast to Rockville, many of the development and rezoning decisions in the area around Gaithersburg in the 1960's have been outside the city limits, and have been made by the county.

By the end of 1965, the county as a whole had almost doubled its 1960 number of apartment units. This doubling had been completed by the middle of 1966 and at that time the number of apartment building permits outstanding was a few more than the number of apartments occupied during the 1960–65 period. In addition, an unknown, but substantial, number of building permit applications had not been processed. Table 4 summarizes the major trends within the county. In order to clarify this summary it is necessary to outline some of the main developments which occurred during the period, especially with respect to zoning.

At the time of the 1960 Census, more than two-thirds of all apartments in the county were in the Silver Spring–Takoma Park area just outside the District of Columbia, and another one-fifth were almost as close to the District in the Bethesda–Chevy Chase area. During 1960 and 1961, these two areas received most of the additions, though some substantial groups were built somewhat further out in Wheaton and much further out in Rockville. Beginning in 1963, and accelerating in the next two to three years, apartment completions spread out much further. The two inner areas, which accounted for over 85 pe cent of the apartments in 1960 and over 60 per cent of the new building in 1960–62, received just under 24 per cent of the units completed between January 1963 and June 1966. However, the shares of Rockville and Gaithersburg declined. (Of the 429 built in the Gaithersburg area in 1966, three-quarters were outside the corporate limits.)

Virtually all the apartments which were occupied by the middle of 1966 were of relatively low density. The zoning ordinance permitted a maximum of 43.56 units per acre. Although there were some high-rise apartments they were still within this density. All could be said to provide a way of life that was intermediate between really high-density apartments in downtown areas and single-family houses. During 1964, the Maryland National Capital Park and Planning Commission[4] began to receive applications to build "apartment hotels" in areas zoned for commercial use. It was possible, under the zoning ordinance, to build apartments on such land without the normal controls over density, height, setback, and site coverage as long as 10 per cent of the units were available to transient tenants—hence the "hotels" part of their

4. The Commission serves the two counties which comprise the Maryland part of the metropolitan area. All of the technical planning and zoning work is done by the staff of the Commission. The Commission itself, appointed by the Governor, then advises the County Council on zoning and planning matters. The recommendation of the staff, along with that of the Commission, is forwarded for use in public hearings.

name. After some delay the County Council amended the ordinance, but not until applications for permits to build several thousand apartments on commercial zoned land had been received.

At the time of writing (late 1966), an unknown number (but certainly over 1,000 units) were represented by permit applications which had not been processed because it seemed unlikely that they would be built, and some permits which had been issued seemed likely to lapse.

Of the 18,155 units in permits outstanding for apartment buildings in June 1966, 11,493 were in apartment hotels. By late 1966, some 2,276 units (7 buildings) had been completed and were at least partly occupied (though they were not on the Assessor's rolls in June), and 11 buildings containing another 4,582 units were under construction. For the first time apartments could be built in the county at densities which permitted builders to bid for the high-cost sites in or near important suburban centers. Of the apartment hotel units for which permits had been issued, 81 per cent were for buildings in the Silver Spring–Takoma Park and Bethesda–Chevy Chase areas and most were close to the commercial centers of those areas. While large numbers of permits were being issued for apartment hotels, permit activity in Gaithersburg and Rockville almost stopped, and the volume of activity in garden apartments on the outskirts of the built-up area continued at about the same rate. The net result was that Silver Spring–Takoma Park and Bethesda–Chevy Chase had nearly regained their dominance in the market. Some 60 per cent of the total outstanding permits were for units in these areas.

In some respects the apartment hotels can be regarded as a second generation of apartments, though many residents hope that the generation will be strangled as soon as possible after birth. In other ways it is useful to consider them as the appearance in suburban centers of the kind of high-density apartments that had previously been confined to the city center. In any case, their role in the accommodation market has been recognized and, at the time of writing, the county had introduced a type of zoning which permitted the construction of high-density apartments in suburban commercial areas, and ensured much more control over them.

A secondary source of information about individual apartment developments in the metropolitan area was *Multifamily Housing 1966*, published by the Division of Planning, Fairfax County. This listed all apartments in the county, including those under construction as of July 1966. The list includes, with a few exceptions, site area and the size distribution of units. For Montgomery County, the air line distance of each building from the District of Columbia was measured. For Fairfax, centrality was measured as the distance from the Federal Triangle of the census tract in which the building is located.

With this broad picture as a background, we can now look at the boom in apartment construction in general as a prelude to a more particular examination of the suburbs. Chapters 3 and 4 contain a more detailed analysis of the nature of the apartment boom in suburban areas and an attempt to explain why it occurred and why it has taken on the characteristics observed.

chapter 2

SOME REASONS FOR
THE APARTMENT BOOM

In this chapter the recent upsurge in the apartment market is examined in more detail and some tentative explanations are offered for its timing. A good deal of literature, dating mainly from the beginning of the 1960's, has attempted to explain the increase in apartment building which began in the late 1950's and, as Table 1 demonstrates, shows little sign of slackening.[1] In the early 1950's, when analysts were trying to find explanations for the opposite trend, it was commonplace to point to increasing income, combined with a high income elasticity of demand for site area.[2] It was then believed that only poor people plus a few sophisticated rich city dwellers lived in apartments. Yet, with income rising rapidly during the 1960's, an increasing number of people were choosing to live in them. Nor was it just that more were joining the ranks of the rich cliff dwellers, because many of the apartments were not even in the central cities. There are, of course, many advantages to apartment life, but if they are to be used to explain the boom they must be shown to have become more important around 1960, or else people must suddenly have become more aware of them.

For example, on the supply side, building regulations and differences in building codes between local jurisdictions increase building costs.[3] Since apartments are large-scale operations, the cost per dwelling unit of adapting to local regulations and negotiating with inspectors is smaller. But, apart from the fact that tract building of single-family houses can also be on a very large scale, there is no evidence that building regulations suddenly began to have this effect around 1960. Complex building regulations may encourage the building of apartments

1. For instance, see Wallace F. Smith, *The Low Rise Speculative Apartment*, Research Report No. 25 (University of California, Center for Real Estate and Urban Economics, 1964); Louis Winnick, "Rental Housing: Problems for Private Investment," *Conference on Savings and Residential Finance, 1963* (Chicago: U.S. Savings and Loan League, 1963); John W. Baird, "National Apartment House Market Outlook," *The Appraisal Journal*, Vol. 32 (1964), pp. 209–13.

2. The best known treatment of the decline of apartment construction in the 1950's is Louis P. Winnick, *Rental Housing: Opportunities for Private Investment* (McGraw-Hill, 1958). The same kind of belief about effects of rising income is reflected by William Alonso in "The Historic and Structural Theories of Urban Form," *Land Economics*, Vol. 40 (1964), pp. 227–31, and in his book, *Location and Land Use: Towards a General Theory of Land Rent* (Harvard University Press, 1964).

3. Advisory Commission on Intergovernmental Relations, *Building Codes: A Program for Intergovernmental Reform*, Report No. A28 (Washington, January 1966).

relative to houses but they did not cause the change in proportions between 1956 and 1960.

Apartments, like offices, but not so much like houses, have always been subject to periodic overbuilding followed by a period when vacancies fall and the pressure of demand builds up. One partial explanation for the boom of the 1960's is that just previously offices had been overbuilt. There was a considerable amount of unused building capacity that was geared to large buildings and builders were prepared to accept low profit margins as long as they could make use of their capacity and skills. In addition, the same lenders who made the office building boom possible were looking for borrowers. Insurance companies and other large institutional investors were prepared to lend up to a very liberal proportion of the anticipated market value of the finished apartment. In Washington, some buildings that were under construction for offices at this time were adapted during the process and finished as apartments.

Demographic Factors

Changes in age structure and in household formation have been favorite explanations for the boom. They can be subdivided into a number of categories. Since they have been analyzed elsewhere they can be treated quite briefly here.[4]

Age composition of the population.   During the 1930's birth rates were very low, but during World War II there was an upsurge which continued after the war. The boom in single-family housing in the 1950's was partly attributable to the bumper crop of babies of the 1920's who were coming into their late twenties and thirties, the peak ages for buying houses. At the same time there was a dearth of young married couples and single people in their late teens and early twenties, who comprise a large part of the apartment market, and are assumed to spend some years in an apartment until they can afford to buy their own house. Around the late 1950's, World War II babies started to make their presence felt and in the early 1960's began to flood into apartments. Between 1960 and 1965 there was a 27 per cent increase in the 15–19 year age group, a 23 per cent increase in the 20–24 year group, a 4 per cent increase in the 25–29 year group, and a 6 per cent decrease in those in their 30's.[5]

4. L. Jay Atkinson, in "Long-Term Influences Affecting the Volume of New Housing," *Survey of Current Business*, Vol. 43 (Nov. 1963), pp. 8–19, details their effects on total housing demand. Wallace F. Smith, *op. cit.*, spells out their implications for rental housing. See also *Savings and Loan Fact Book, 1966* (Chicago: U.S. Savings and Loan League, 1966), pp. 21–26.

5. U.S. Bureau of the Census, *Current Population Reports*, P 25, No. 329 (March 1966).

The elderly also favor apartment living and they, too, comprise a rapidly growing group. If age composition is an important reason for trends in housing types, it is possible to go quite far in forecasting what will occur in the near future. As the babies of the 1940's continue to come into the market they will maintain a strong demand for apartments. Toward the end of the decade they will begin to make their presence felt in the house market and in the 1970's will cause a very strong resurgence in the demand for houses. But unless and until the very recent fall in birth rates affects the numbers of late teenagers, we can expect a continued strong demand for apartments as both the young and the old grow in numbers. This kind of demographic trend implies a shift in aggregate demand but it does not imply a change in taste or a shift in individual demand curves.

Household formation. A second trend which has operated in the same direction over a longer period does imply a change in taste, although it is probably closely related to income. Atkinson[6] points out that up to 1940 the relationship between numbers of households and numbers of adults in the population was fairly steady. For each twenty adults there were about nine households. But since then the addition of 25 million to the adult population has produced 18 million more households. This in turn is the result of a number of reinforcing trends. An increasing proportion of males of each age group are married. Since household formation traditionally follows marriage, this produces more households. The Census Bureau, projecting these trends into the future, estimates that the proportion of males between 20 and 24 who are married will increase from 43 per cent in 1960 to 48 per cent in 1975. For all males in their 20's, the proportion will rise from 73 per cent to 76 per cent. Cross-sectional studies show that low-income males are more likely to remain unmarried, so that an income factor seems to be at work here.

But even young persons who do not marry are more likely to be able to set up a separate household when incomes are high. Whether they are at college or working, young persons in an affluent society are more likely to live in apartments and less likely to live with their parents or in an institution. Between 1950 and 1960, the number of primary individual households increased by more than 60 per cent. There is a point, of course, where these factors work in opposite directions. If most young people in their late teens and early twenties comprise primary individual households, the more of them who marry, the fewer the number of households. Each marriage reduces the number of households by

6. Atkinson, *op. cit.*

Table 5. Trends in Apartment Size: Suburban Washington

(Per cent)

	Before 1960	1960	1961	1962	1963	1964	1965	1966ᵃ	Permits	Totalᵇ
Arlington County										
Efficiency	8.1%	19.6%	17.8%	25.0%	13.2%	32.0%	23.9%	23.5%	—	13.8%
1 Bedroom	51.4	50.0	43.0	39.8	40.7	37.8	42.2	34.0	—	48.4
2 Bedroom	36.8	27.9	34.8	31.3	46.1	28.2	25.2	32.2	—	34.3
3+ Bedroom	3.7	2.6	4.4	3.8	0	2.0	8.5	9.3	—	3.7
Alexandria County										
Efficiency	—	3.6	0	0.6	13.6	15.7	17.8	19.6	—	14.5
1 Bedroom	—	32.6	34.4	40.9	42.3	40.6	41.0	35.8	—	39.7
2 Bedroom	—	51.0	51.0	46.8	35.8	25.7	35.7	35.3	—	35.5
3+ Bedroom	—	12.8	14.6	11.7	8.3	18.0	5.5	9.3	—	10.3
Fairfax County										
Efficiency	0.6	0	3.0	5.4	0	2.2	4.0	0.7	—	2.5
1 Bedroom	30.9	0	39.3	49.1	36.0	31.3	35.0	39.2	—	36.5
2 Bedroom	60.6	0	47.0	40.3	59.1	60.9	47.4	44.3	—	51.6
3+ Bedroom	7.9	0	10.7	5.2	4.9	5.6	13.6	15.8	—	9.4
Montgomery County										
Efficiency	1.3	0.4	0.7	1.0	0.6	6.6	0.2	6.1	19.8%	7.8
1 Bedroom	44.4	26.2	24.2	33.9	47.1	40.1	36.0	29.9	43.9	40.4
2 Bedroom	46.0	60.3	60.3	51.2	45.6	44.6	52.9	41.4	28.8	41.9
3+ Bedroom	8.2	13.2.	14.8	13.9	6.8	8.8	10.9	22.6	7.6	9.9

ᵃ First six months only.
ᵇ Totals for the years and categories shown (includes permits for Montgomery).
– Not available.
Note: Totals do not always equal sums of items, due to rounding.
Sources: Arlington: Office of Planning, Arlington, Va., Apartment Development by Census Tract (1965, and supplement to mid-1966). Alexandria: Alexandria Department of City Planning and Urban Renewal, "Size of Apartment Units," Information Bulletin No. 2 (July 1966). Fairfax: Department of Planning, Fairfax, Va., Multifamily Housing 1966 (1966). Montgomery: Unpublished material and Maryland National Capital Park and Planning Commission, Apartments and Their Impact on the Public Elementary Schools, Technical Bulletin No. 10 (July 1959).

one. On the other hand, if the majority of marriages are between people who are not living alone, they increase household numbers.

This trend in household formation is of long standing. Its significance for the apartment market is that it is most marked among those who, because of age and family structure, tend to live in apartments. Thus, it has reinforced the change in age structure. If early marriage is followed by early parenthood, and if high incomes allow the young family to buy a house at an early age, they may move out of apartments more quickly. This could reduce the effect of early household formation on apartment demand. At the other end of the life cycle, the number of households has also grown as widows and widowers find it financially possible to live alone rather than with their children. Divorced and separated individuals can also manage to maintain a household rather than return to live with parents or other members of their families.

These demographic changes are widely held to be important, but I know of no attempt to estimate quantitatively how important they are. The main problem with such an analysis would be the lack of data on the family composition of new apartment dwellers. Probably most primary individual households and young married couples live in apartments but there is no data to show just how many of the newly constructed apartments are occupied by them.[7] The 1960 Census is too far out of date and no large special surveys have been conducted. The Bureau of the Census has plans to carry out a special survey which should provide useful information for this purpose.

Tables 5 and 6 contain information which indirectly reflects the influence of demographic factors on the apartment market. Assuming that the family structure of households living in apartments remained the same, it would be expected that apartments would tend to become gradually larger as incomes rose. They might have a larger floor area without any change in numbers of rooms, or the number of rooms might increase. But the upsurge in demand for apartments implied by an increase in the proportion of single persons and married couples would be expected to have the opposite effect, provided, of course, that the proportion of family-size apartments rented by groups of unrelated individuals is not increasing. Since there is no data for the District of Columbia or Prince Georges County, nor for Alexandria apartments built prior to 1960, and for only about two-thirds of Montgomery

7. Anshel Melamed, in "High Rent Apartments in the Suburbs," *Urban Land,* Vol. 20, No. 9 (October 1961), quotes figures from an unpublished thesis by Wm. Frankel, "Why People Who Live in Suburban Apartments Prefer the Suburban Environment to a Downtown Apartment," (University of Pennsylvania, Wharton School, 1961). Only 2-1/2 per cent of the household heads were less than 34 years of age. But high rent suburban apartments are, as Melamed points out, a very special class, and in 1960 the upswing in suburban apartments had barely commenced in Philadelphia.

Table 6.   Schoolchildren per 100 Apartment Units:ᵃ Montgomery County

Date apartment built	Number of schoolchildren in:		
	Elementary school	Junior high school	Senior high school
1959 Survey:			
Before 1960	19.0	—	—
1966 Survey:			
1960	17.6	6.7	6.0
1961	33.1	8.5	2.5
1962	21.8	6.4	4.6
1963	12.6	3.5	4.5
1964	11.5	2.8	3.5
1965	12.0	2.5	1.7
1966	9.9	4.8	3.6
1960–66	16.9	4.8	3.6

— Not available.
ᵃ The low numbers shown confirm the common view that families living in apartments have fewer children, at least of school age, than families in single-family houses. In a "Report on a Study of Elementary School Needs with Total Land Development of the Colesville Hillandale Area" (Rockville, Md., 1964), the County School Board assumed 80, 27, and 5 elementary school pupils per 100 single-family houses, garden, and high-rise apartments, respectively. The assumption is based on survey results.
Sources: 1959 Survey: Maryland National Capital Park and Planning Commission, *Apartments and Their Impact on the Public Elementary Schools,* Technical Bulletin No. 10 (July 1959). 1966 Survey: Montgomery County School Board records.

County apartments, they do not provide a very convincing test of the significance of demographic influences.

The figures in Table 5 present a mixed picture. Since Arlington and Alexandria have increasingly become locations for central area type apartments, it is not surprising that an increasing proportion of smaller units has been built in both. In Montgomery, the apartments built in the first three years of the 1960's were distinctly larger on average than those built prior to 1960. But since then the trend has been in the opposite direction though, apart from the permits outstanding, the proportion of efficiency and one-bedroom apartments has not been as high at any time between 1960 and 1965 as it was prior to 1960. Among the apartment hotels which are now being built in the suburban centers, the proportion of small units is much higher. Fairfax appears to have experienced a definite, though uneven, trend toward smaller units.

Perhaps the income effect is being felt most strongly at the other end of the size range. In each of the areas, the proportion of units with three or more bedrooms is surprisingly high and appears to have increased since before 1960 even though the proportion of efficiency apartments has also been increasing. The strong increase in the proportion of small apartments in Arlington and Alexandria during the 1960's and in Fairfax since before 1960 is consistent with a strong demographic influence in the apartment boom. Perhaps Montgomery County, by 1966, was just beginning to catch up with this trend through its apartment hotels.

The conclusions to be drawn from Table 6 are even less definite. In 1959, a fairly comprehensive survey of Montgomery County apartments found an average of 19.2 elementary schoolchildren per 100 units. In 1966, a survey of about 60 per cent of the apartments built since the beginning of 1960 found an average of 16.9 elementary schoolchildren per 100 units. It is difficult to change the size of apartments once a project has been built but the number of children fluctuates with apartment age, demand conditions, and specific management policy. The slightly smaller number of elementary schoolchildren per apartment in the later survey is very weak evidence that an increasing proportion of apartments are occupied by childless families or individuals. In fact many would argue, and Table 6 supports the argument, that as apartments get older the numbers of children increase. However, in 1966, a resurvey of somewhat over one-third of the apartments surveyed in 1959 showed that the number of elementary schoolchildren had decreased from 700 to 600.

Unfortunately, there is no historical record of the number of schoolchildren in higher grades. Table 6 suggests that the average age of children may increase somewhat as apartments age. Many children of less than school age may also live in the apartments. Like the data on apartment size, these figures can only be said to be consistent with, though they do not strongly support, the hypothesis that demographic changes have been a major factor in the apartment boom.

Mobility and the House Owner as Speculator

There can be no doubt that one of the attractions of house ownership is that, in growing metropolitan areas, it is possible to reap handsome capital gains if and when the house is sold, and at worst it is a good hedge against inflation. Both house and land prices tended to rise more rapidly than the general price level during the late 1940's and early 1950's, but it is widely believed that during the late 1950's and in the 1960's the rate of increase has slackened, although it is difficult to collect firm evidence on this because the statistics that are available are not very suitable. Between 1960 and 1964 the average value per square foot of floor area of existing houses insured by the FHA increased by only 5.35 per cent; and for the Washington SMSA, by only 7.25 per cent.[8] For a four-year period these increases are small, though there is no assurance that the figures are for houses that are comparable in other respects.

Another trend that is widely believed to be important is increasing family mobility. In Washington one is particularly aware of high mobility. However, throughout the United States there has been no marked change in the frequency of moves since the first mobility survey in 1948. Between 18 1/2 per cent and 21 per cent of the population move to a different house, and between 5 1/2 per cent and 7 per cent move to a different county, annually.[9] The costs of making a real estate transaction have certainly not been falling over the period since 1950 and the family that found it profitable to buy a house (even if they had to sell it in, say, five years) in the 1950's may prefer to rent in the 1960's. A large number of single-family houses are, of course, available for renting even though very few are built with long-term renting as the objective.[10] For example, house owners who are temporarily transferred may rent rather than sell their houses. But the number of such houses is so limited that a family deciding to rent is partly pushed into the apartment market, as well as being attracted by the advantages of apartment living.

This might be a "chicken and egg" kind of argument. It could be argued that softness in the market for houses has resulted from the swing towards apartment living. The speculative motive of house owners could reinforce the downward trend in the relative prices of houses, if one exists. Most analysts claim that if speculators operate profitably they tend to stabilize a market, by buying when the price is low and expected to rise, and selling when the price is high and expected to fall. But the house owner does not have much choice about when to buy and sell. He is limited, as a rule, to a decision between buying or renting, or between selling or renting. For many homeowners the choice is even narrower. If they do not sell their old home when they move they will not be able to afford to buy a new one. Given the constraints under which decisions are made and the length of the period of the fluctuations (if they are fluctuations and not a reversal of a trend), the specula-

8. Federal Housing Administration, *FHA Homes: Data for States and Selected Areas* (Washington, 1960 and 1964).
9. U.S. Bureau of the Census, *Current Population Reports,* P 20, No. 150 (April 1966).
10. Row houses ("town houses" in the new real estate terminology) are quite often built for rental purposes. They are one-family houses by the census definition, and are treated as such in most of the analyses in this volume. But in terms of density they are intermediate between garden apartments and detached houses. The Montgomery County data in this study include a small number of town houses.

tive motive for owning a home could as easily increase as reduce the amplitude of long period fluctuations, and can certainly reinforce a trend.

Relative Building Costs

One possible explanation for the increased popularity of apartments is that they have become cheaper to build, relative to houses. Building apartments is a relatively large-scale operation and a casual observer sees a great deal more use of cranes, mechanical lifts, and other modern machinery than in house building. But the opinion of people close to the industry is that there has been much less than a revolution in techniques of building, even of high-rise apartments. Garden apartments are built in much the same way as houses. Industrial methods of building have had the effect mainly of lowering the costs of fixtures and joinery, and this has been as helpful to the large-scale house builder as to the apartment builder. Such advanced techniques as modular construction are much less common here than in Europe.

This judgment is borne out by the Boeckh Index of Construction Costs. Figure 2 shows how this index has behaved since the end of World War II. Unfortunately, apartments are lumped together with offices and shops. But the index suggests that the cost of constructing a standard type of apartment has, in fact, risen slightly more rapidly than the cost of building a standard type of single family house. One of the disadvantages in using this type of index is that the standard "basket" for which it is constructed soon becomes out of date. A rather different

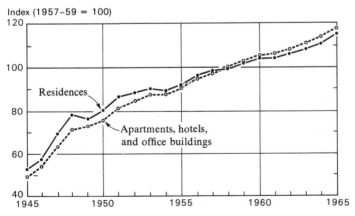

Figure 2. **Boeckh indexes of dwelling unit costs (1957–59 = 100). Source: E. H. Boeckh and Associates, Inc., and U.S. Department of Commerce, reproduced as Table A49 in U.S. Department of Housing and Urban Development, Housing Statistics, Annual Data (May 1966).**

picture emerges from Figure 3. Here the Census Bureau's average estimated construction cost per unit can be seen to rise much more rapidly
for single-family houses than for apartments. Between 1947 and 1957,
single-family construction costs rose by 93 per cent and multifamily by
31 per cent. Between 1957 and 1965 the increases were 25 per cent and
7 1/2 per cent respectively.

But it is difficult to interpret a series which is not adjusted for quality
changes at all. The relative fall in apartment construction costs since
1957–58 could be a result rather than a cause of the upswing in apartment construction. If the small number of apartments that were built
in the early 1950's were predominantly large high-cost apartments in
central areas, and the upswing took the form of providing more of the
smaller and cheaper apartments, the apparent fall in relative cost could
be due to falling relative quality rather than falling costs for constructing
the same unit. Table 5 presented some evidence of a trend towards
smaller apartments in the Washington suburbs. Although construction
costs do not include land prices, the trend toward suburban apartments
would also reduce construction costs, as high-rise construction is more
expensive than low-rise. But this does not explain the long-term tendency during the 1950's for unit costs of one-family houses to rise three
times as fast as unit costs of apartments, when the market share of
apartments was falling.

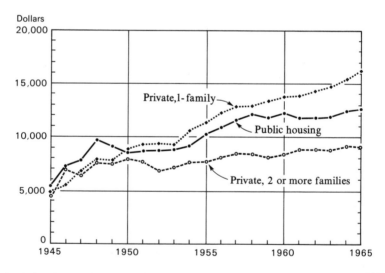

Figure 3. **Estimated construction costs of non-farm starts. Source: U. S. Department
of Housing and Urban Development, Housing Statistics, Annual Data (May 1966),
Table A5. The old series figures (before 1959) have been linked to make them comparable with the new series. The difference is small.**

Public housing costs have followed a trend intermediate between private homes and private apartments. Between 1947 and 1957, unit costs rose 51 per cent, and between 1957 and 1965, 9 per cent. Most public housing is high-density construction in central areas, and there is no reason to believe that it has changed very much in quality over the period considered. Apartments have probably been providing an increasing share of the low-cost housing units built since the mid-1950's. At the same time, of course, the rapid rise in single-family house costs suggests that they were increasingly confined to a higher income sector of the population.

Areas in which apartments appear to have gained during the period are in the range of facilities they have begun to provide and the range of types of apartments that have come onto the market. Developers have begun to exploit the advantages of collective living. It is possible to provide better recreation facilities, child care, and air conditioning more cheaply in apartments than in single-family dwellings. The product has become more varied in that builders have been providing the whole range of locations, floor areas, associated facilities, and services. While more efficiency units have been built, the numbers of 3- and 4-bedroom units have also been increasing. It is now possible to rent apartments ranging from the very cheap to the very expensive, and to choose those features and a location that are especially attractive.

Basically, apartments are more suited to providing this type of range than single-family houses, partly because they can be provided collectively and partly because, with variable density, they can compete for all but the very choicest commercial sites. Since apartment developers have only recently begun to take advantage of these possibilities, they may be regarded as innovations on the supply side. It is impossible to decide whether the innovations met a previously existing demand, or whether the demand for this type of facility grew very rapidly. Using data from the Chicago and Detroit transportation studies, Kain[11] showed that apartment dwellers who work in the suburbs are much more likely to live in the central area than are house dwellers. This suggests that at that time there was a demand for apartments in a particular location (the suburbs) which was not being met.

Income Tax Provisions

The combination of accelerated depreciation of apartment buildings for tax purposes and the concessional capital gains tax has produced a

11. John F. Kain, "The Journey to Work as a Determinant of Residential Location," Regional Science Association, *Papers and Proceedings*, Vol. 9 (1962), pp. 137–60; and John R. Meyer et al., *The Urban Transportation Problem* (Harvard University Press, 1965), Chapter 6.

tax advantage for apartments which at least partly offsets the long-standing advantage of single-family house owners in not paying tax on the imputed rent of their dwellings.[12] Since 1954 it has been permissible for the first owner of an apartment building to depreciate it for tax purposes at double the straight line rate, applied to the declining balance. Wallace Smith gives an example of how this works. A building which costs $100,000 and has an expected life of forty years would normally be depreciated at 2 1/2 per cent each year. But accelerated depreciation permits a depreciation of $5,000 the first year, 5 per cent of $95,000 the second year, and so on. Subsequent owners of the property can depreciate at 1 1/2 times the straight line rate, on the declining balance.

For the long-term owner the advantage is largely that taxes can be postponed since the absolute amount of depreciation computed by the accelerated method will fall below that computed by the "straight line" method ($2,500) after fourteen years. However, this can be well worth while since the tax saved can be reinvested. If an enterprise grows rapidly enough, and is willing to reinvest its revenue rather than pay out dividends, it need never pay any taxes. The higher the income tax bracket of the developer, the greater the advantages. For someone paying 50 per cent tax at the margin there will be an increase in after-tax income of $1,250; an increase of 1 1/4 per cent in the rate of return on the total capital. But if, as has been common, the developer was able to borrow, say, 90 per cent of the total cost, the tax saving represents an increase of 12 1/2 per cent on the rate of return on his equity. This is clearly enough to affect the level of investment. Accelerated depreciation is available whether or not the property is earning any net income. It can be offset against the developer's income from other sources. The tax shelter provided is so valuable that developers have been prepared to accept quite high vacancy rates to get it.

Accelerated depreciation is very valuable to the owner who sells the apartment after some seven to ten years. Until 1964 it was possible for the seller to treat the difference between the sales price and the depreciated value as a capital gain. If the property was kept for this length of time, the Internal Revenue Service regarded it as a capital gain rather than regular income. This was then taxed at the concessional capital gains rate which is, in effect, half of the rate which would apply if it were

12. Tax advantages for apartment builders are discussed by Wallace F. Smith, *op. cit.*, pp. 31–34; Sherman Maisel, *Financing Real Estate* (McGraw-Hill, 1965), Chapter 14; and R. Bruce Ricks, *Recent Trends in Institutional Real Estate Investment*, Research Report No. 23 (Center for Real Estate and Urban Economics, University of California, 1964), pp. 10–11, 88 ff. On the value of non-taxation of imputed rent, see Richard Goode, "Imputed Rent of Owner Occupied Dwellings Under the Income Tax," *Journal of Finance*, Vol. 50 (1960), pp. 504–30. This subject is examined again in Chapter 8 of the present study.

treated as income, with a maximum of 25 per cent. Since 1964 it has only been possible to treat as a capital gain the margin of the sales price above the original value depreciated at normal (not accelerated) rates. The developer can still count on the use of the tax savings until the time of the sale. If he sells within a shorter period he can only use the concessional capital gains tax if he has "amateur status" for tax purposes. One consequence has been an influx of doctors, lawyers, and other professional and business people into apartment development. As long as they do not engage in it too frequently they can make use of both the tax shelter and the capital gains concessions. Both of the tax advantages are greatest for people with a high marginal income tax rate. Sometimes real estate operators have acted as managers of a development for a syndicate which put in the equity capital plus its members' amateur tax status. Smith has shown that there is a good deal of this type of financing in California and my own observations suggest that it is important in the Washington area.

In Chapter 1 it was suggested that the role apartments play in urban development makes them peculiarly suited to a developer who wants to take much of his return in the form of capital gains. A very large-scale development in effect creates an increase in the value of land and a small scale development can take advantage of the expectation that changing circumstances will make the area more valuable. Because apartments are rented rather than, like homes, sold as soon as they are completed, an apartment developer has more time to back his own estimate of the pattern of future urban development by holding the property while the appreciation he anticipates occurs. In some degree he takes his returns as capital gains rather than income, and in some degree capitalizes on his special knowledge of future urban development.

Although the accelerated depreciation provisions were new in 1954, the capital gains concession was not. The latter cannot help to explain the upsurge in profitable apartment development, but when other circumstances were favorable, it contributed to an increase in its volume. Smith[13] points out that, when mortgage finance is freely available, it is possible for a developer to finance virtually all of his cash costs by borrowing. In effect, he sells the property without paying tax on the gain in value which has occurred. Having covered his financial costs in this way, he cannot lose and can still gain by selling later at a price which exceeds cost. This is an extreme example of the gains that can be made when credit conditions are such that the capital gains and the tax shelter all accrue to the owner of a small equity in the project. But the

13. Smith, *op. cit.*

investment of the time and skills of the developer are genuine opportunity, even if not cash, costs. Smith also mentions a way to avoid the
taxation of capital gains even when a property changes hands. If an
owner trades the property for another of a similar kind, it is not necessary to declare the proceeds of the sale for tax purposes. As long as the
profits remain in the development enterprise they are not taxed.

Changing Tastes

If changing population characteristics and relative cost trends (as a
result of changing supply conditions) do not explain the increase in
apartment living, there must have been a change in the preferences of
consumers of housing. At present we can do little more than speculate
in this area. The results of one survey[14] indicate that there has been no
decline in the desire of the typical American family to live in a suburban home or in its willingness to accept long journeys to work if they
are necessary. One way to test whether there has been a change in
tastes, as distinct from changes in age distribution and family structure,
would be to find out whether there is an increase in the proportion of
families living in apartments, when stratified by age and family structure.
Families with more than one child and with a household head in the
30–55 age group would be of particular interest. This sort of analysis
could be carried out on the 1960 *Census of Population* data and compared with the data which the Census Bureau proposes to collect during
a special survey of apartments in the near future.

The changing family structure could possibly reflect a change in taste
toward apartment living. The argument would be that people like living
in apartments and therefore decide not to live with their parents or (in
the case of the elderly) with their children. This is another supply and
demand kind of interaction, but the change in family structure is more
likely to be the basic underlying cause and the demand for apartments
the result, rather than vice versa.

Many urbanists and planners would like to find evidence that the
trend toward apartment living indicates that city dwellers are at last
coming to terms with city living rather than trying to compromise between urban and rural by living in the suburbs on their own pieces of
land. This might be happening because many of the young people now
forming families are urban born and reared, and do not look back nos-
talgically to a childhood in the country. This wishful thinking has a flaw:
a high proportion of the apartments are being built in the suburbs

14. John B. Lansing and Eva Mueller with Nancy Barth, *Residential Location and
Urban Mobility* (University of Michigan, Survey Research Center, 1964), especially
pp. 42–49.

rather than near the commercial and cultural heart of the cities. Moreover, many of them are at very modest densities, and are neither very close to the centers of employment and retailing that do exist in the suburbs nor within walking distance of either suburban services or public transport. From observation, the rate of car ownership is relatively high.

But, without being starry-eyed about it, there are signs that acceptance of a higher living density does indicate that some of the attractions of what Australians call "the cult of the quarter acre" are palling. Even though many of the apartments do have a considerable open area around them, often with a swimming pool, tennis courts, and playground, they require a degree of communal living which the true suburbanite would not tolerate. Some of the open space provides facilities which substitute for the urban park as well as for the back yard. And again some quite high-density apartments are very much like downtown apartments, being built in the larger suburban centers. These will be looked at more closely when the trend to suburbanization and towards the fringes of the suburbs is examined.

There does appear to be a growing willingness among older people to live in apartments rather than try to maintain houses that are larger than they need, and become an increasing burden in terms of finance and responsibility. Suburban apartments are particularly attractive to them, especially if they have retired, do not need to travel downtown to work, and wish to stay close to their children and their friends.

Perhaps, contrary to Lansing and Mueller's[15] findings, more and more people are deciding that the choice between high land prices in the inner suburbs and long trips to work from the fringe do not present alternatives that are as attractive as an apartment which is both convenient and inexpensive for the facilities provided. They are willing to substitute communal space for private back yards and often inaccessible public parks. If these factors are important, we would expect apartments to be more common in the largest cities and in cities where land prices are highest. Rapidly rising land prices could favor house buying if they were expected to continue, or discourage it if they were not, or if potential buyers were more impressed with the higher cost of accomodation in a single-family house than with the speculative gains. Increasing land prices might be a greater attraction to apartment than to house owners.

It is not difficult to think of reasons for preferring apartment living. There is little risk of a very large financial cost, either from selling the property in a hurry in an unfavorable market, or from unforeseen re-

15. Lansing and Mueller, *op. cit.*

pairs, taxes, or high utility bills.[16] There is much less uncertainty, more freedom to come and go when you please, and no work to do in maintaining the structure, or in keeping the yard in order. Perhaps even more attractive than not having to do these tasks or paying to have them done is not having to worry about them.[17] Owning a house has often been the one investment which the family of modest means made, and managing the investment has been regarded as an enjoyable enterprise. But it seems to be becoming more and more common for the ordinary family to own stocks and shares. Especially through syndicates, they find that it is easy to own real estate, even if they rent an apartment. Although none of these attractions suddenly became important in the late 1950's, many of them had been neglected when the obituary of apartment living was being written in the earlier years of the decade.

We simply do not know whether, given age and family circumstances, and the same choice between apartments and homes, the family of the 1960's would be more likely to choose to live in an apartment than would its equivalent in the early 1950's. To find out would require much more statistical material than is at present in existence, and even then it may not be possible to separate all of the influences satisfactorily.

16. Most apartment rentals, at least in the Washington area, include the cost of all utilities except telephones.

17. In a survey of planned communities it was found that, except in the low price bracket, one of the most important attractions of town houses compared with detached houses was that no outside maintenance, especially yard maintenance, was required. Common open space and recreation facilities were attractions of these communities to all residents. The survey found higher mobility in town house communities than in those with detached houses. *Open Space Communities in the Market Place*, Technical Bulletin No. 57 (Urban Land Institute, 1966).

chapter 3

APARTMENTS
IN THE SUBURBS

It is difficult to define just what is meant by an apartment boom *in the suburbs*—or at least to show statistically whether or not there has been one. Although the central city has recognizable features, it is not easy to delimit it or to show precisely how it changes in area over time. Partly in recognition of this, and partly because it would not be practicable to change boundaries frequently, the statistical central city of each SMSA is a fixed area that corresponds to the boundaries of a local government jurisdiction. In a growing city the central area would also be expected to grow, and sometimes it is known to shift.[1] If central area land uses spill over into suburban areas, there can be a very large statistical increase in suburban apartment building without an increase in the area that is truly suburban.

In the Washington SMSA there can be little doubt that there has been a boom in suburban apartments (see Table 3), though this has also been accompanied by rapid building of apartments in the District of Columbia. In 1960, the District accounted for 62 per cent of the metropolitan area's housing units in structures containing three or more units. During the first half of the 1960's it only attracted between 15 per cent and 30 per cent of gross increases, as shown by permits issued. Only a part of the difference spilled over into the close-in suburbs of Arlington and Alexandria, which together accounted for 17 per cent of the area's apartment units in 1960. During the early 1960's these suburbs issued from 10 per cent to 25 per cent of the area's permits for multiple-family dwellings, despite an increase in the number of permits issued in the District from an annual level of just above 2,000 in the first two years of the decade to over 8,000 in 1965. There seems, then, to be some justification for talking about a boom in the building of apartments in the suburbs and for regarding this as a special feature of the 1960's.

Migrations to the Suburbs

Probably suburban apartments can best be considered in the general framework of the "suburbanization" of metropolitan areas. Many of the reasons that made, first, the single-family house owner, then the shop-

1. For a study on Philadelphia, see John Rannels, *The Core of the City* (Columbia University Press, 1956).

ping center developer and the manufacturer, and lately more and more office occupants, migrate to the suburbs have also induced the apartments dweller to leave the central city. These migrations have been documented and analyzed extensively,[2] and explanations for them range from the obsolescence of the central city's buildings, streets, and subdivisions, to racial factors. In this chapter some of these reasons are examined in more detail. Each of the migrations reinforces the others: people living in apartments may be attracted to suburban areas because they are quite likely to work there; their families and friends probably live there; shopping in the suburbs is often nearly as good, and much more convenient, than downtown; and the suburbs now can even boast good cultural facilities. On the reverse side of the suburban explosion is the slow rate of redevelopment of downtown areas. The suburban apartment is often a substitute for a downtown apartment in a redevelopment area. One way to ask why so many apartments are being built in the suburbs is to ask why they are not being built more rapidly in more central areas. Perhaps our society is the urban equivalent of nomadic agriculture. We exploit an area and then move on, rather than replace old buildings and old street patterns.

Suburban apartments demonstrate the inadequacy of simple models in which the downtown area is the center of attraction and other land uses are clustered around it in rings of both decreasing density and decreasing land value.[3] Once a city reaches a very modest size this pattern is disturbed by at least three factors. The first is that the city center exists only because of economies of scale and because the functions it performs are concentrated together. The city does not have to become very large before some of these functions can be duplicated and a pattern of suburban service centers appears, very similar in arrangement to the hierarchies of central places spread throughout the country.

The second factor is that traffic congestion increases near the city center so that distance and accessibility are no longer proportional. It becomes much quicker and easier to get to a suburban shopping center, even if it is no closer than the central business district (CBD). This is not just because too little has been invested in roads, although road

2. George Sternlieb, "The Future of Retailing in the Downtown Core," *Journal of the American Institute of Planners*, Vol. 29 (1963), pp. 102–11. The detailed findings of the New York Metropolitan Region study are summarized by Raymond Vernon in *The Changing Economic Functions of the Central City* (Committee for Economic Development, 1959).

3. This is the basic model used by Lowdon Wingo, Jr. in *Transportation and Urban Land* (Resources for the Future, Inc., 1961), and by William Alonso, in *Location and Land Use: Toward a General Theory and Land Rent* (Harvard University Press, 1964).

space is expensive in central areas. Smeed[4] has shown that in large cities which rely on automobiles, the area required, both for driving with tolerable congestion and for adequate parking space in the city center, would be so extensive that distances within the center, including walking distances, would become uncomfortably large. Even if a large city were to be designed from the start with an optimal system of transport, there would be an important role for suburban centers. This role is made more important because we choose to travel in space-consuming automobiles rather than walk and use public transport as our grandparents did.

Without making any judgment as to whether the provision of roads has been too slow or too fast, it is worth asking what effect a more generous road program would have had on the extent of suburbanization. When the earliest suburbs were being built, the difficulties of getting into the city for virtually everything that the suburbanites wanted, including employment, must have been a severe disincentive, so that better roads would have hastened the growth of suburbs, as the long-run model implies. But once the suburbs reached some size, the difficulties of getting to the center prompted retailers, and then various other services and manufacturing industries, to locate in the suburbs—first to take advantage of the market that could be tapped, and then of the labor force that could be attracted. During this phase, better roads would have slowed down the growth of suburban employment and services. The last phase occurs when a high proportion of the purchasing power and the labor force is located in the suburbs and the center finds it difficult to be more than a local shopping and employment center for the relatively poor people who live nearby, and a place to shop at lunch time and on their way home from work for those who are still employed there. It tries to attract customers and employees from the suburbs. In this phase, again, good roads contribute to the relative health of the central city.

Third, a long-run model has serious drawbacks because most cities adapt slowly to changing conditions and very seldom start afresh with the redevelopment of areas of any significant size. As a consequence, the buildings and streets, transport services, and public facilities in the older sections of cities are more or less obsolete. Since the city centers are generally the oldest parts, this is an additional reason why they frequently lose business and population when they are in competition with suburbs.

4. R. J. Smeed, "The Traffic Problem in Towns" [paper read before the Manchester Statistical Society (England), February 8, 1961].

William Alonso[5] has pointed out that the voracious space demands of an increasingly affluent society led to the migration to the suburbs of the post-war period. To some extent, though, this migration had a push as well as a pull element. The continued inmigration of low-income groups from rural areas and overseas helped to push the middle-income family out of its city house, or at least allowed it to sell without sustaining too heavy a loss. The fact that many of the new inhabitants of the inner city were Negroes tended to push the migration faster and made the inner city an even more unattractive environment for many whites.

With this general picture of the process of suburbanization, we can consider in more detail some of the possible reasons why so many of the new apartments are in the suburbs. It is difficult to show, quantitatively, that some of the reasons suggested have had a significant impact. Certain elements of policy cannot even be documented, as they are the opinions of people close to, and operating in, the field.[6] This chapter deals only with what effects policies might have had. Chapter 8 is devoted to an evaluation of whether the effects are desirable or not. The reasons for building apartments on the suburban fringes will be considered in Chapter 4.

The Slow Rate of Redevelopment in Central Areas

The mirror image of the fast rate of development of the suburbs is the slow rate of central area redevelopment. This is not a new phenomenon nor is it confined to apartments. Central areas have received an even smaller proportion of new houses than of new apartments. Once an area is fully urbanized a new single-family house can be built only if an old one is pulled down to make room for it, and there is no net change. But apartments can compete with commercial land uses. Demolition of a few houses or low-density apartments can make room for a large number of high-density apartments. Because the housing in these areas is old, and because its density is quite high, poor families can afford to live in it, even if under crowded conditions, despite the fact that the land is relatively valuable. The land in areas of old housing near the city center is not nearly as valuable as its closeness to the center would suggest, largely because of the kind of environment created by poor families living in old housing. Any redevelopment that does occur spreads slowly out from the center, or from established

5. Alonso, *op. cit.*; and Alonso, "A Theory of the Urban Land Market," *Regional Science Association Proceedings* (1960), pp. 149–57.
6. Although I interviewed quite a large number of people and read transcripts of zoning proceedings, it would be necessary to carry out a far more detailed examination of policy making before any firm conclusions could be reached.

centers of redevelopment, along main arteries. Families that are displaced cannot afford the new accommodation (except public housing) and are pushed into other areas.

The crowded, old housing is not only occupied by poor families supported by low-wage earners. Many people who live there do not have jobs, either because of disability, lack of basic skills, or their own preferences. Many criminals, social misfits, disabled people, broken families, and alcoholics are found there. There is also a noticeably high proportion of Negroes. As a result, many people find apartment living in the central area attractive only if they can afford to live in new apartments and have incomes and ways of life which allow them to isolate themselves from their surroundings. Central city living is unattractive to those who feel unsafe in the street at night and to families which do not wish their children to mix or go to school with slum children. The slow rate of redevelopment of inner cities is partly caused by these factors.

The larger the area of high-income housing in the inner city, the less important are the slums, although it seems unlikely that high-income housing can ever be completely isolated from the slums. Most slum families cannot afford new housing anywhere, particularly on high-valued land. The environment may be improved in some respects when they are rehoused in subsidized public housing, but the population density may not be increased. If it is not, the pressure will remain for higher-income families to move to the suburbs as poor families take over new parts of the city.

A more efficient way to deal with the problem of a poor environment in the city is to assist families which cannot afford better housing, either through rent subsidies or through some kind of guaranteed income. Even rent subsidies would be treating a symptom of the problem rather than its cause. Unless their spending is closely controlled, recipients of subsidies will spend less of their own income on rent than previously and increase their housing standards by less than the subsidy would allow. In any case, attempts to make them spend more on rent rather than increasing their total welfare would seem to be ill advised.

Racial Discrimination

The effects of racial discrimination on housing patterns have been the subject of a number of studies.[7] When Negro families are not permitted to buy or rent housing in relatively high-cost areas, even when they can

7. See, for example, Davis McEntire, *Residence and Race, Final and Comprehensive Report to the Commission on Race and Housing* (University of California Press, 1960); Otis Dudley Duncan and Beverly Duncan, *The Negro Population of Chicago* (University of Chicago Press, 1957); and John R. Meyer, John F. Kain, and Martin Wohl, *The Urban Transportation Problem* (Harvard University Press, 1965), Chapter 7.

afford to, the pressure on the housing stock in the areas they can occupy is increased. They are admitted to housing in poorer areas and
their bids increase the price which poor families have to pay and make
it more profitable to keep slum property than to redevelop or renovate
it.

Although there is evidence in the opposite direction, some of the
data presented by Meyer, Kain, and Wohl[8] imply that racial discrimination may be stronger in multiple-family than in single-family housing.
They show that Negroes working in outer areas are quite likely to be
able to live in houses near their work, but are much less likely to be
able to live in apartments outside the central area. This is consistent
with the view that discrimination is aimed at avoidance of contact with
Negroes. Contact is much closer between families in an apartment,
especially a garden apartment, than between families which live in
houses in the same area. Even a small ghetto of Negro houses can be
quite effectively isolated, but in an apartment isolation is more difficult.

If the high-income Negro sector of the population becomes large
enough, it might be expected to stimulate some redevelopment within
the areas it occupies. But many of these families want the kind of low-
density living in the suburbs which is denied them through discrimination, and which they cannot afford on the high-valued land of the
ghetto. Racial discrimination is very much a part of the general problem
of the slow rate of inner area redevelopment. Some white people regard
a large Negro population as an unattractive feature of an environment,
quite apart from its other undesirable features.

Local Government Revenue and Expenditure

Since central cities and suburbs are very commonly controlled by
different local governments, there are differences in their levels of
services and levels of taxes and charges. Most observers believe that the
central city has become less attractive over time because of its role in
the metropolitan area.[9] Its expenses have been heavy and have increased rapidly: slum dwellers, almost by definition, require heavy
expenditure on welfare, police, and fire protection services. If it is to
maintain anything like its traditional dominance in the metropolitan

8. Meyer, Kain, and Wohl, op. cit.; figures 22 and 23 show that non-whites employed in the suburbs are much less likely than whites to live close to their work,
if they live in an apartment. For workers in single-family houses, the racial differences are much smaller.
9. For example, Harvey E. Brazer, "Some Fiscal Implications of Metropolitanism,"
in Guthrie S. Burkhead (ed.), Metropolitan Issues: Social, Governmental and Fiscal
(Syracuse University, Maxwell Graduate School of Citizenship and Public Affairs,
1962); Seymour Sacks, "Metropolitan Area Finances," in Proceedings of the Fifty-
Sixth Annual Conference on Taxation . . . 1963 (Harrisburg, Pa., 1964).

area, the city must provide cultural, recreational, and other "public goods" for the whole metropolitan area, and it must provide roads for access to the CBD and parking space for cars when they get there.

But the central city has had to rely on property taxes to provide a very large part of the funds for these purposes, and the property base for the tax has been growing quite slowly. One response has been to increase rates, even though this might aggravate the problem by discouraging the very developments that would increase the base for the tax. At the same time the level of services that the city can provide for its own residents has not risen as rapidly as in the suburbs, making it less attractive for those who can afford (and whose skin color will allow them) to live elsewhere. Thus schools in central cities are often poorer and parks are too few.

There has been a good deal of discussion about whether property taxes have a significant effect on the volume of building in a local government area. It seems to be difficult to demonstrate this effect in cross-sectional studies that compare areas where the rate of taxation varies,[10] apparently either because the property tax differences are so small as to be subliminal, or because they are so overwhelmed by other differences that their effects cannot be distinguished. But there are strong intuitive grounds for believing that they do have a significant effect, at least in states where property tax rates are high.[11] The fact that at least three states have taken steps to lessen the burden of property taxes after redevelopment suggests that they may have an effect on the rate of redevelopment. There is a good deal of debate about whether abatement of part of the property tax in New York has had any significant effect on the rate of redevelopment. The New Jersey concessions are too new to assess and the concession given in Boston was a particular arrangement for a single project.[12]

In the Washington SMSA, differences in the rate of property taxation are not significant, but differences in the level of services certainly are. Most schools in the District of Columbia are regarded as distinctly inferior to most of the suburban schools because of lack of funds. As a

10. Morris Beck, *Property Taxation and Urban Land Use in Northeastern New Jersey* (Washington: Urban Land Institute, 1963); M. Rawson, *Property Taxation and Urban Development* (Urban Land Institute, 1961); Dick Netzer, *Economics of the Property Tax* (Brookings Institution, 1966), Chapter 4.

11. M. Mason Gaffney, "Property Taxes and the Frequency of Urban Renewal," in W. Kress (ed.), *Proceedings of the Fifty-Seventh Annual Conference on Taxation . . . 1964* (Harrisburg, Pa., 1965).

12. Dick Netzer, *op. cit.,* pp. 83–85; Morris Beck, "Urban Redevelopment: Influence of Property Taxation and Other Factors," *Proceedings of the Fifty-Seventh Annual Conference on Taxation . . . 1964.* The effects of the tax on rehabilitation and maintenance are discussed in detail by James Heilbrun, *Real Estate Taxes and Urban Housing* (Columbia University Press, 1966).

result many white families send their children to private schools so that, compared with 60 per cent of the District's population, 85 per cent of its public school pupils are Negroes. The District is poorly provided with parks and recreation areas and other services do not measure up to the levels of the suburbs.

Land Speculation and Zoning Policies

One of the major attractions of the suburbs to the apartment developer has been that he could make profits out of land speculation, especially in areas where the local planning authorities have been cooperative in granting rezoning. Even if there had been no zoning control over land use, the suburbs would still have offered a more attractive opportunity for making profits from the increases in land values that a developer anticipates—and helps to bring about if his project is large enough. To the extent that he can influence other public and private land users, his profits can be made higher. The suburbs have a considerably more rapidly changing land market than inner areas. It has been much easier to acquire the necessarily fairly large tracts of land in the suburbs, since there has not been the fragmentation of ownership that has occurred in the slums. Former owners of undeveloped land in the suburbs have been willing to sell for a share of the spoils without any of the resettlement problems of the inner city. Nor has the suburban apartment builder been forced to compete for land with slum families willing to pay quite high rents for the existing buildings. The interests of the suburban farmer or land speculator and the apartment developer conflict only in the matter of dividing the profits. But the interests of the apartment developer can be opposed to those of the slum dweller, if not to those of the slum landlord.

In suburban municipalities there has been a conflict of interest between apartment developers on the one hand, and house owners on the other. Although house owners have very frequently made the political headlines, highlighting the deleterious effects of apartments on the neighborhood, pointing to traffic congestion, overcrowded schools and recreation facilities, and the fact that their reasonable expectations about the future character of the area will not eventuate,[13] it often seems that the developer has actually won the rezoning decision. Perhaps this has been a result of the political power of individual devel-

13. "Apartments in Suburbia: Local Responsibility and Judicial Restraint, a Symposium," *Northwestern University Law Review*, Vol. 59 (1964), pp. 344–432; Howard J. Grossman, "Apartments in Community Planning: A Suburban Area Case Study," *Urban Land*, Vol. 25 (January 1966).

opers, who have a much greater stake in the outcome than any single house owner.

In Montgomery County, Maryland, in the 1963–66 period it seems to have been relatively easy to have land rezoned for apartments.[14] In fact, it appeared that the legal costs of a good zoning lawyer could possibly be regarded as the cost of getting rezoning. Land already zoned for apartments was relatively unattractive because its owners had already put a premium on their selling price, but land zoned for single-family housing or even for agricultural purposes could be bought much more cheaply, even if the purchase was, as quite commonly, conditional upon rezoning being granted. As long as the area could be construed as in some sense suitable for apartments, there would be a good chance of rezoning being granted, at least in the 1963–66 period.[15] It almost appeared that the best way to keep apartments out of an area was for the Planning Commission to take the initiative in rezoning it for apartments—the current owner would then reap the capital gain and the area would be made less attractive to apartment builder-speculators. Of course, this was an unstable situation and resulted from the expectation that the liberality of the rezoning policy would not continue. The political opposition to it was ample justification for this belief.

Despite the arguments about overcrowded schools and roads, there is a good deal of evidence that apartments, compared to single-family houses, do in fact contribute more to revenue than to public expenditure.[16] Certainly zoning lawyers have frequently claimed this in applying for rezoning. They may well have convinced the government bodies who make the decisions that rezoning would reduce the level of taxation on the rest of the community.

As of August 1, 1959, if the whole area in the county zoned and not used for apartments had been used up to the maximum density allowed in each particular zone, it would have accomodated 12,800 apartment units. The 1960 MNCPPC report,[17] claimed that this was too much, in relation to the rate of use, and that it gave the community too little control over the rate and location of apartment development. It was

14. These conclusions are based on opinions. Statistics of the fraction of applications granted are valueless, as developers and lawyers will only make application where their chances of success are quite good.

15. This was the term of office of the County Council. The effects of its policy on numbers of applications for, and granting of, rezoning is reflected in the fact that between 1958 and 1962, 215 acres were rezoned for apartments or town houses. Between January 1963 and June 30, 1964, 666 acres were rezoned. At least in part because of public dissatisfaction with this policy, only one incumbent Council member was renominated for the 1966 elections, and none were re-elected.

16. This point will be returned to in evaluation of policy in Chapter 8.

17. Maryland National Capital Park and Planning Commission, *Residential Land Use: A Preliminary Plan* (Silver Spring and Riverdale, Md., 1960).

Table 7. Changes in the Capacity of Apartment-zoned Land: Montgomery County, 1959–1966[a]

Year	At beginning of period				Changes in capacity of vacant land during period		Smoothed rate of building	Number of years' supply of vacant zoned land at current bldg. rate[b]
	Capacity of vacant land	Units on Assessor's rolls	Total capacity	Per cent used	Additions by rezoning	Deletions by building		
	(....Dwelling units....)							(Years)
August–December 1959	8,474	12,355	20,829	59	1,780	812	1,561	5.4
1960	10,254	13,167	22,609	58	4,256	2,716	2,205	4.7
1961	14,510	15,883	26,865	59	1,353	1,763	2,011	7.2
1962	14,700	17,646	28,218	63	3,622	1,800	1,696	8.7
1963	15,922	19,446	31,840	61	11,969	1,419	1,679	9.5
1964	26,472	20,865	43,809	48	10,858	2,078	1,965	13.5
1965	35,252	22,943	54,667	42	7,652	2,285	3,060	11.5
January–June 1966	40,619	25,228	62,319	40	8,776	2,597	—	—
July 1966—period when all permits have been used	46,793	(34,081)[c]	71,095	39	—	—	—	—

[a] Excludes municipal areas of Gaithersburg and Rockville.
[b] Capacity of vacant land/smoothed rate of building (at beginning of each period).
[c] At end of period.
Sources: Maryland National Capital Park and Planning Commission, A Preliminary Master Plan of Residential Land Use (Silver Spring and River-dale, Md., July 1960); Assessor's rolls; building permits; rezoning records.

estimated that there was sufficient capacity to last through 1980 if there was no rezoning. The rate at which this capacity has been added to by rezoning is compared to the rate at which it has been reduced by apartment building in Table 7. The figures exclude the cities of Rockville and Gaithersburg (total vacant capacity in 1959, 4,333 units; leaving 8,474 in the rest of the county), each of which controls its own zoning. It also excludes from the numbers of building permits outstanding those which are to be built on land zoned for commercial uses; i.e., the apartment hotels.

The construction of Table 7 has only been possible by using some quite heroic approximations. The entries are based on the assumption that all land zoned for apartments will be built to the maximum density ✓ allowable in each zone. Developers nearly always get close to the maximum. The figures have been extracted from records of rezoning, building permits, and assessments, most of which had to be taken at their face value. One source of error is that rezoning deals with gross areas, whereas building permits and assessments deal with areas net of public roadways. The starting point is August 1959, but it is not known precisely which areas were considered vacant at that date, especially areas for which building permits had been issued and on some of which buildings were under construction. The additions to, and substractions from, the vacant apartment-zoned land refer only to the August to December period. In the table it was assumed that all apartments which came on to the Assessor's rolls between August 1959 and December 1960 were under construction, and these were regarded as "used" in the 1959 figures.

In order to get some indication of whether speculative holding of vacant apartment-zoned land increased in this period, the stock at the beginning of each year is compared with the rate at which the capacity of vacant land decreased through building. This was a period of increasing apartment construction and at least some of this increase could easily have been anticipated by looking at trends in building permits issued, and, less accurately, by getting the feel of the market. The county councilors could be expected to take account of building trends when considering rezoning applications. To avoid some random fluctuations, the current rate of building in year t is smoothed by calculating $0.25 B_{t-1} + 0.5 B_t + 0.25 B_{t+1}$, where B is the number of units entering the Assessor's rolls during the year. The 1965 figure is probably high because it is based on the assumption that another 2,600 units will be added to the Assessor's rolls in the second half of 1966. The capacity of vacant apartment-zoned land, varying with the permitted density, is then expressed as a number of years' capacity at the current rate of use.

The 50 per cent rise in smoothed rate of building for 1965 is probably exaggerated and the apparent fall in the number of years required to use all the vacant zoned land should not be given too much weight.

The capacity of apartment-zoned land is added to by the net rezoning for apartments, usually from land zoned for single-family houses, but also by the rezoning of agricultural land and existing apartment-zoned land to permit higher densities. Applications are received in May and November each year and most are dealt with in the following six months. It is assumed that capacity is added in year t if the application was made in November of year $t - 1$ or in May of year t. In June 1966, quite a number of the November 1965 applications had not been decided, so the rezoning figures for the first half of 1966 are underestimated relative to previous periods.

There is no clear optimal relationship between the rate at which apartments are being built and the capacity of vacant land. It appears to take at least a year from the time a rezoning application is lodged until a building permit is issued; i.e., time to deal with the application for rezoning, prepare the permit application, and have it dealt with. Because of the way in which Table 7 has been prepared, this would appear as an average of 0.25 years of vacant capacity (none for applications lodged in November and 0.5 years for those lodged in May). At least another year elapses before the building comes on to the Assessor's rolls and few buildings appear before 30 months after the rezoning application is lodged (this justifies 21 months vacant capacity in Table 7). The larger the building, the longer each of these delays will be, and it can be expected that financing and other arrangements will stretch them in some cases. However, a planning authority which wished to use its rezoning powers as a means of keeping fairly close control over the location of apartments would probably not have more vacant land zoned for apartments than would satisfy the next three years' requirements of builders. This would include land on which apartments were under construction.

The greater the value in the last column of Table 7, the less control the rezoning authority has over apartment location. For instance, if there is a 12-years' supply of vacant land, developers as a group have the choice of at least four sites for any site which may be developed. This kind of elbow room opens the door for speculator-developers to play a larger role, and is evidence that they are exerting a greater influence on the determination of the pattern of growth. If they are to make the best use of their skills as judges of what future developments will take place, and to be able to induce the most favorable development of surrounding facilities, they need to be able to hold on to their land for a considerable time between rezoning and building.

Unfortunately, I was not able to trace through in detail the history of plots that had been rezoned to find out about transactions, the provision of urban facilities, and whether there was any difference in the time lag if a developer or some other land owner actually went through the process of getting the land rezoned. Whatever one's judgment about the proper figure for the supply of vacant land available column, it clearly increased spectacularly during this period, permitting those developers who had their land rezoned to get returns from increased land values, some of which were passed on to the occupants of their apartments in lower rentals. If most developers get their land rezoned, competition between them will force rentals down and rezoning can be regarded as a lower cost strategy than the alternative of buying land already zoned for apartments.[18]

The history of apartments built on land zoned for commercial uses—apartment hotels—has been outlined in Chapter 1. In this case the relatively favorable attitude of the County Council to the land development interest was evident in the delay between the recommendation from the Planning Commission that the ordinance be amended to control this type of development, and when it was amended. The apartment hotel boom has shown that there is a demand for apartments at a high density in suburban areas and a new zoning—category R-CBD—has been introduced to permit them in prescribed central business districts within the county.

A controversy over sewer location in the other suburban Maryland county (Prince Georges) highlighted the fact that the Planning Commission does not have effective control over the location of water and sewerage facilities in the two Maryland suburban counties. Tannian[19] has shown this in some detail in his examination of the operations of the Washington Suburban Sanitary Commission. The commission seems to have been very willing to extend water and sewer facilities to new developments in the two-county area. Frequently it charged much less than the full cost of the service extensions and, despite requirements for consultations and for approval of its program of extensions,[20] it seems to have been willing to extend services even into areas where master plans called for low-density development. Once the sewers are in, possibly

18. That there were any gains to be made was again a result of the fact that it was anticipated that rezoning would become more difficult in the future with a change in county government. In the long run, apartment-zoned land was expected to be a scarce commodity. However, the extent to which this shortage would be reflected in rentals in the short run depended on the rate of building.

19. Francis X. Tannian, "Water and Sewer Supply Decisions: A Case Study of the Washington Suburban Sanitary Commission" (Unpublished Ph.D. Thesis, University of Virginia, 1965).

20. Recent legislation gives the County Council a veto over its decisions.

to serve one large customer, it appears to have been politically impossible for the county to refuse rezoning for much higher-density uses.

In an environment so favorable to developers, the returns to be made from increases in the value of land often outweighed the net returns from the apartments themselves. In Montgomery County, at least, this seems to have encouraged apartment developers to place their apartments in the county, rather than in adjacent parts of the District, where it may have been more difficult to get favorable decisions.

I have produced no reasons to explain the large increase in suburban apartments at the particular time it occurred. Rather I have tried to show that when the apartment boom occurred, the conditions were relatively more favorable in the suburbs than in the central areas.

chapter 4

APARTMENTS ON
THE SUBURBAN FRINGE

One feature of the apartment boom of the 1960's which is particularly surprising to a casual observer is that some apartments are being built on the fringe of suburban development. In this chapter, some possible reasons for this are suggested and the experience of the Washington SMSA is examined to determine, first, the extent of fringe apartment building and, second, whether the Washington experience fits in with the suggested explanations. However, I must admit that few of the causal hypotheses are tested satisfactorily.

In the analysis of this trend I have had to rely almost entirely on two sources of data for the Washington SMSA: the 1960 census tract data for the SMSA and subsequent building within each tract, and the data on individual apartments built and permits issued in Montgomery County. Some information on individual projects in Arlington and Fairfax counties, in the Virginia part of the SMSA, is also available. However, it is very difficult to measure the trend within the suburbs toward fringe areas, both because some of the fringe areas of 1960 were well inside the fringe in 1966, and because there has been a tendency for apartments to be built further from the District of Columbia boundary with time. But this would still be the case if the proportion of apartments in fringe areas had remained the same while the location of the fringe itself moved outward.

One significant result of the analysis of Montgomery County apartments is the change that seems to be occurring in this movement away from the city center (see Table 4). When unweighted data were used for each project in Montgomery County, there was a trend away from the District boundary (correlation between building date and distance from the District = 0.224).[1] But if data for building permits outstanding are added, the time trend almost disappears, $r = 0.015$. One reason for these low values is that Gaithersburg (13 miles from the District) has apparently pursued a policy of encouraging the development of garden apartments and there has been a steady demand for them throughout the period (probably from people employed nearby), though Gaithersburg contains the most distant (from the District of Columbia) significant

1. The data used are described in Chapter 1 and the precise definition of the variables is given later in this chapter (pp. 72–73) where the data are analyzed more extensively.

concentration of apartments in the county. Rockville, the county seat, is closer (8 miles) and has also been able to attract a steady flow of apartment development. In 1959, one-third of the apartment-zoned land in the county was in these two corporate areas which pursue independent planning and zoning policies. For Fairfax County the time trend was rather more strongly away from the center of Washington. The simple correlation coefficient between distance and year in which building was commenced was 0.373.

Urban Expressways and Market Differentiation

During the 1960's there has been a rapid growth of urban expressways, making areas quite remote from suburban centers easily accessible to them in terms of travel time. In the Washington area the single most important stimulus to this type of suburban apartment was the building of the Capital Beltway. The map of Montgomery County on page 15 shows the apartment projects of the early 1960's strung almost like beads along either side of the main highways.

The traditional picture of apartment dwellers as having few cars and being within walking distance of employment and shops, or close to public transport, has become obsolete, partly as a result of the apartment boom. Developers have been catering to families who are as mobile as the house owner. In fact they may be much more mobile, since they are not tied to home by the need to look after house and grounds, and are less likely to be tied to children. Interested as they are in being able to get quickly to many parts of the city and to other cities, in the Washington SMSA these people are more attracted by access to the Beltway than by closeness to shops. They also need parking space, and this can be provided more cheaply where land prices are lower.

Apartment developers appear to have been very active in exploring the variety of the kinds of apartments that could be marketed successfully. One type is the luxury apartment in an area with very good recreation facilities. It may be high-rise, like the Washingtonian Towers just south of Gaithersburg which is in the middle of a golf course. Or it may be a private garden apartment in which no children are permitted, like the Parkside Apartments just outside the Beltway on Rockville Pike. At the other end of the scale, it is probably cheaper to live in a two- or three-bedroom garden apartment on the urban fringe than in a new house with comparable facilities. Even if this involves driving to work, perhaps in a car pool, it can be a very logical housing choice for a young family. In addition, many of the occupants are accustomed to the suburban environment, having grown up there, and consequently the fringe suburban apartment, as a step towards a house, has very strong attractions.

Location of Employment

The Beltway has attracted many employers as well as apartment developers. There are some very large employers in Montgomery County, though a good number of the largest date from before 1960 when approximately 40 per cent of the employed persons who lived in the county also worked there. At that time most of the large employers were located in or close to the major suburban centers, a high proportion of them being engaged in retailing and services. Even the large government employment centers were close to the commercial centers. Although there has, since 1960, been a considerable expansion of office employment, especially in Silver Spring, there has also been a very large growth of employment in wholesaling and light manufacturing, much of it in the so-called knowledge industry. These firms have tended to concentrate in fringe areas, especially between Rockville and Bethesda. This area (Grosvenor–Twinbrook district) contained 280 apartment units in 1960 and had added another 3,000 by mid-1966, at which time permits were outstanding for another 2,900 and enough land was zoned for apartments to accommodate a further 13,000.

apartment dwellers from having to live as close to their employment or

Although a relatively high rate of car ownership and use has liberated to public transport as used to be necessary, they still probably live closer to their work than the home owner. Table 8 contains information derived from transportation studies. It can certainly be regarded as predating the present apartment boom, and therefore should be interpreted with care. However, it is quite clear that at this time people living in outer suburban apartments were more likely to work in the outer suburbs than those living in outer suburban houses. This applied only in the two outermost rings in Detroit and the three outermost in Chicago. It is interesting to note that two-family house dwellers have more in common with apartment dwellers in this respect than with people living in single-family housing. In fact, in Chicago's outermost areas, they were more frequently employed in the outer area than were apartment dwellers. In some respects the garden apartment is a direct descendant of the row house and duplex. Certainly relatively few of the latter were being built in the 1960's.

With the progress of time, the relationships shown in Table 8 may have been weakened, though not necessarily so. Meyer, Kain, and Wohl[2] report a good deal of reverse commuting by people living in apartments in inner areas and working in outer areas, perhaps because

2. John R. Meyer, John F. Kain, and Martin Wohl, *The Urban Transportation Problem* (Harvard University Press, 1965), Chapter 6.

Table 8. Frequency of Local Employment

City and ring of residence	Employed in same ring as residence			Employed in same or adjacent ring		
	One-family	Two-family	Multiple-family	One-family	Two-family	Multiple-family
Detroit						
2	29.71	34.30	32.13	78.31	78.19	79.10
3	40.97	42.68	42.44	80.87	82.89	78.95
4	29.18	32.25	29.26	68.86	67.42	67.08
5	24.93	32.66	28.00	55.05	60.23	61.27
6	27.58	46.80	51.74	45.82	60.44	66.87
Chicago						
1	45.39	44.52	41.58	75.34	76.14	74.31
2	30.45	30.02	30.81	69.49	74.14	71.76
3	32.59	30.35	26.58	62.52	64.41	57.35
4	28.43	27.80	26.25	56.20	55.40	49.81
5	27.29	41.43	35.07	53.10	65.56	58.70
6	26.83	40.93	43.48	51.60	65.57	63.51
7	35.45	69.50	59.41	47.72	81.97	71.57

Note: Because of small numbers, residents in the CBD (ring 1 in Detroit, ring 0 in Chicago) were omitted.

Source: Tabulations from unpublished material collected for the Detroit (1953) and Chicago (1956) Transportation Studies, by John F. Kain. I am grateful to him for making these available to me. For maps, see Meyer, Kain, and Wohl, *op. cit.,* pp. 124, 125.

there was an insufficient supply of apartments in outer areas. The 1960's may have partly met a pre-existing demand from people already working in the suburbs who wanted to live in apartments closer to their work.

Retirement Communities

These communities contain mixed housing, but with a relatively high proportion of garden apartments and town houses. In Montgomery County, Rossmoor Leisure World has completed the first sections of its 900-acre development. The county introduced a special zoning category, Planned Retirement Communities (PRC), which permits up to 10 dwelling units per acre compared with 12 1/2 for normal town house zoning and 14 1/2 for the lowest density apartments. But the area also contains recreational facilities, such as a golf course, and a few commercial buildings. Although it would seem that the occupants by definition would not be interested in nearness to employment centers, applicants, in fact, need only be over 52 years of age, and many expect to work for a number of years. But the orientation is to the years of retirement.

These apartments are just a special case of differentiating the product to appeal to particular tenants. Most of the retirement communities have been built relatively close to metropolitan areas, but far enough away to allow a large area of land to be bought at a modest price. Many of the tenants are likely to have ties—families and friends—with the adjacent suburban areas.

Utility Policy

The willingness of the Washington Suburban Sanitary Commission to extend water and sewer service to new apartment developments without necessarily recovering from the user the full cost of the extension, thus removing a discouragement to fringe apartment location, was noted in Chapter 3. Telephones and electricity are also connected to new developments on the fringe without charging the full cost of extensions to the system, but this is probably of less significance. These policies in general aid the extension of single-family homes on the suburban fringe at least as much as apartments, but if the demand for apartments is taken as given, they favor suburban developments.[3]

A study[4] of land prices in northeast Philadelphia estimated that land with access to sewers is about twice as valuable as otherwise comparable land. The proportionate increase was somewhat greater for land zoned for higher-density row housing than for detached single-family dwellings. In fact, within any zoning category, access to sewers was easily the most significant factor affecting land price at any given time.

Zoning

One explanation for the trend toward fringe development that immediately springs to mind is zoning policy. Before the appearance of apartment hotels, the highest density at which apartments could be built anywhere in Montgomery County was 43.5 units per acre (one unit per 1,000 square feet). The allowable density appears to control rather closely the price a developer is willing to pay for land. Both government assessors and lenders value apartment-zoned land at so much per unit permitted, adjusted for the location of the site.

Variations in density alone account for a little under half (48 per cent) of the variations in assessed unit land value between different apartment sites. The value of R^2 rises to 0.605 when the additional explana-

3. In Chapter 7 the features of a utility pricing and investment policy which would contribute to optimal allocation of land are discussed in more detail. Actual policies are compared with the ideal in Chapter 8.

4. Grace Milgram, "Transactions, Prices and Development of Land in an Urbanizing Area of Philadelphia, 1945 to 1962" (University of Pennsylvania, Institute for Environmental Studies, August 1966).

tory variables—i.e., distance from the District, and date of building—
are included. The equation (with standard deviations shown in parentheses) is[5]

Unit value = 16,740 + 537.0 Density − 164.8 Distance
                         (55.0)   (32.5)
−1,512 Date built (1960 = 0)
   (369)

The negative trend with date since 1960 is not easy to explain unless it
reflects the fact that, even given distance from the District boundary,
changes in micro-location have occurred over time.[6] A decreasing proportion of apartments have been close to commercial centers.

It appears that during the first half of the 1960's the two main commercial centers in the county, Silver Spring and Bethesda (the area either
side of Wisconsin Avenue from the District boundary to the National
Institutes of Health) developed to such an extent, with land values increasing correspondingly, that builders of apartments at a density of one
unit per 1,000 square feet could not afford to buy land. There is very
little vacant land in these centers and it may be possible to use that
which does exist for higher-density commercial purposes. In addition,
there are very few low-valued houses, except very close to commercial
development, where commercial land use is also possible. It is not
profitable to buy sound single-family houses for demolition in order to
build apartments at these low densities. This is particularly true if the
land has a possible commercial potential, and if there are problems in
assembling a large enough site for a viable project.

When the demand for high-density apartments became strong enough
it became profitable for developers to bid for land actually zoned for
commercial uses, because the zoning ordinance permitted apartment
hotels without density limits, thus allowing them to compete with commercial users. Some of the highest land prices recorded in the county
($10–$20 per square foot) have been paid by these developers. The
assembly problem also becomes much less important: at densities of
hundreds of units to the acre, a viable project can be built on a small
area. One result is an almost complete gap in densities between about
43 and 120 units per acre. It is too early to assess whether the demand
for apartment hotels is large enough to fill all that are being built. The
first building was quickly rented, but three more recently completed are

5. These variables are defined on pp. 72–73.
6. Note that this regression excludes permits outstanding for which there are no
land value figures. Hence, it does not reflect at all the recent return of apartment
building to suburban centers in the form of apartment hotels.

reported to be less successful. It is difficult to avoid the feeling that, when projects presently under construction are completed, the commercial difficulties will increase substantially.

The importance of zoning is highlighted by comparing these two areas with the immediately adjacent areas across the District of Columbia boundary. In both cases, the areas inside the District have relatively few apartments. In Bethesda there are few jobs within walking distance of the apartments being built at the District boundary. The main attractions seem to be the currently good bus service to downtown Washington and the expectation of a rapid transit station at the District boundary. But these would have been at least as strong if the apartments had been built in the District. Perhaps Maryland is attractive because its residents have a vote in local, state, and congressional elections. It is unlikely that families living in these apartments are attracted by Montgomery County's good schools because, at such high densities, and with little or no outdoor space, few of them are likely to have children. Certainly race is not currently relevant because the adjacent areas of the District have very few Negroes. Differences in zoning policy seem to be the main reason. The District has been less willing to zone these outer parts for high-density apartments.

The previous chapter alluded to the willingness of the County Council to rezone land for apartments. The greatest part of that land has been in fringe areas or was in vacant lots that were not very close to the main centers. Even if the apartment developer could bid for land near established commercial centers, rezoning for apartments would produce relatively little increase in its value, which might not be enough to pay the legal fees unless a large parcel could be assembled. This is nearly as difficult near suburban commercial centers as it is downtown.

It is rather paradoxical that a phenomenon which is often blamed on lax zoning control—namely, the spread of apartments to the fringes of suburban areas—is at least partly the result of one of the zoning restrictions which has been maintained—the refusal to permit densities greater than one unit per 1,000 square feet of lot. When some way is found to circumvent this density restriction, a new upsurge of apartments close to the city and suburban centers is very likely to occur. This is one of the lessons of the apartment hotel phenomenon in Montgomery County. The Planning Commission recognized this and has made provision for higher-density apartments in the future. Other suburban local governments in the Washington SMSA have also recently introduced higher-density zones for apartments with the special objective of permitting apartments in commercial areas.

Speculation

I use this term to mean the influence on land use decisions of expected future changes in the value of land used for alternative purposes.
The value of land for a particular purpose is the current value of the
expected flow of net returns, and this can change in different ways for
different kinds of land use. But the large-scale landowner can influence
the value of one part of his land by what he does with the remainder.
Then again, the large-scale landowner can anticipate that the way he
uses his land will affect the land use decisions of owners of adjacent
land. Further, he is sometimes in a position to influence both the use of
nearby land and the external constraints on his own land use decisions.

Some of the most important decisions that are external to the individual land owner are taken by government or semi-government bodies.
One is the zoning constraint, another is the investment and the user
charging policy of utilities and government services. By far the most important are sewers and roads. They are both costly to install and essential for development at more than very modest densities. Tannian[7] has
suggested that it is possible for landowner-speculators to influence both
the timing of sewer development and the level of "contribution" which
the user is required to pay for the trunk sewer extension. By hiring a
good zoning lawyer it is certainly possible to influence zoning decisions.
In Fairfax County there have been allegations that developers have also
used bribery to influence these decisions.[8] The same developers, and
one of the same officials, have operated in Montgomery County. Even
without any illegal influence, familiarity with the kind of zoning decisions likely to be made by the county and the kind of sewer supply
decisions likely to be made by the Sanitary Commission becomes one
of the valuable assets in apartment development, like skill in judging
the market and anticipating the direction and timing of future land use
changes.

It is impossible to measure the extent to which the location decisions
of apartment builders have been influenced by the desire to make capital
gains. Without very detailed examination of the price at which land
changed hands, and of the agreements and conditions of those purchases, the importance of this kind of motive cannot even be judged. It

7. Francis X. Tannian, "Water and Sewer Supply Decisions: A Case Study of the
Washington Suburban Sanitary Commission" (Unpublished Ph.D. Thesis, University
of Virginia, 1965).

8. *The Washington Post*, September 21, 1966, carries an account of these allegations which led to indictment of developers, county commissioners, and planning
officials. A recent article by Alfred Balk, "Invitation to Bribery," in *Harper's
Magazine* (October 1966), suggests that the problem is widespread.

would be even more difficult to identify the steps taken by a land owner to influence others in such a way that the value of his land would increase as much as possible, whether the others be private land owners and developers or public or semi-public bodies.

It is also difficult to attribute the speculative motive to individual landowners and developers. A speculator is more interested in the increase in the capital value of his land and less in the steady flow of income from it. But the increase in capital value can be reaped through higher flows of income, and anyway the difference is a matter of degree. The developer-speculator will sometimes build his apartments as soon as zoning and sewerage have been arranged and may keep them for the seven to eleven years that seem necessary to get the best of tax shelter and to avoid having the capital gains counted as ordinary income for tax purposes. Building his apartments early rather than waiting for the surrounding area to become urbanized can be an optimal strategy, even if it is unprofitable in the early years. It has the considerable advantage of preempting a part of the market. Those who hold their land vacant take the risk of being squeezed out of a market of limited size.

This kind of speculation is certainly not related to rapid sale after the profit is made. Those for whom the rise in land values is most important may be those who hold their land the longest, and who even after the apartments are built, still hold for as long as the investor interested in income would hold them.

In Chapter 1, apartments were characterized as a relatively speculative type of residential land use. I cannot prove that conditions in the outer suburban areas were, in the first half of the 1960's, more favorable for the operation of land speculation of the kind I have discussed. However, a good deal of evidence seems to be consistent with the process of land development described. Apartment developers can be attracted to the urban fringe by the increasing value of land during the process of development. By passing on a part of their returns from increased land values in the form of lower apartment rentals, these developers have, in turn, been able to attract tenants. Part of the attraction of the fringe to developers is that it is much easier to assemble the large tracts necessary to maximize speculative profits. Another part is the much greater rate of change in land use, and the accompanying opportunity to shape the external influences on land values. If outer suburban public authorities have been more sensitive to real estate interests in making zoning decisions or in providing public facilities—especially, perhaps, in fringe areas—this would also have contributed to the fringe apartment development.

Washington SMSA Census Tracts

The data in Chapter 1 threw some light on patterns of growth in the housing stock throughout the area. Some of the findings give a more detailed picture of the trend toward a higher proportion of apartments in the suburbs, and of their location within the suburbs. Two major questions were asked of the data. First, where has apartment growth occurred during the 1960–65 period and how does this compare with the location of the stock of apartments and houses in 1960? Second, given the location of the total growth in the housing stock, what factors determine its distribution between houses and apartments? This can also be usefully related to the distribution of the housing stock in 1960. One reason for asking the second question is that it will probably be easier to say something more useful about it than about the first. Since the data available did not include any indicators of the area of land available for new housing in each tract in 1960, there seems little chance of being able to predict where new housing as a whole will be built. But this is part of the task if the first question is to be answered.

The brief answer to the first question is that, since 1960, apartment growth has spread into the suburbs to a very much greater extent than it had prior to 1960. The answer to the second question is less clear. Apartments have continued to dominate the new housing in inner, relatively low-income areas but seem to be following the trend of new single-family housing and moving to the suburbs, although of course they are less dominant there. Transit does not appear to be very important as a locational factor and apartments are certainly not confined to areas with old housing ready for demolition. These general answers are explored in more detail below.

Let h = total number of housing units in the census tract;
   a = total number of apartments in the tract;
   subscript 60 = the housing stock at the time of the 1960 Census; and
   subscript 60–5 = additions to the housing stock during those years.

Once the tracts which were very largely occupied by institutions had been eliminated, the remainder formed a group in which the 1960 number of housing units was of a comparable order of magnitude.[9] It would have been possible to use actual numbers of apartments built during 1960–65 as the dependent variable in seeking answers to the first question. However, it seemed worth neutralizing the dimensional differences that do exist, and the dependent variable is defined as apart-

9. The variance was 1,015 compared with a mean of 2,084.

ments built during 1960–65 (a_{60-5}) divided by the total stock of housing units in 1960 (h_{60}). I have used the term "growth by apartments." Like a number of other variables used in this analysis it has a rather peculiar distribution. The modal value is zero because there were many census tracts in which no apartments were built. However, the mean is 0.196 and the standard deviation 0.445 for the whole SMSA. By comparison, a similarly defined variable, "growth by houses" [$(h-a_{60-5})/h_{60}$], has a mean of 0.137 and a standard deviation of 0.448. The housing stock in the unweighted average census tract grew by about 33 per cent during this six-year period. However, most of this growth was concentrated in tracts which had less than the average number of housing units in 1960. The total housing stock grew by about 27 1/2 per cent.

Since my particular interest is in truly suburban areas I have carried out all of the analyses, first, on all tracts together, and second, separately on the tracts which comprise Montgomery, Fairfax, and Prince Georges counties as one group, and the District of Columbia, Arlington County, and Alexandria as another. Although this does not clearly provide the best division between inner and outer areas, it is convenient. There were some areas of vacant land in the inner areas in 1960, especially in outer Arlington and Alexandria, but this land had been by-passed. There were certainly no large vacant areas, and this is reflected in the building permit figures shown in Tables 2 and 3. The numbers of permits issued for single-family houses in the inner area has been small throughout the 1960's.

The correlation coefficients between the major variables are shown in the matrix. The variables are defined as follows:

X_1 = apartments built during 1960–65 per housing unit existing in 1960 (growth by apartments) (a_{60-5}/h_{60});
X_2 = apartments as a proportion of the net additions to the housing stock 1960–65 (a_{60-5}/h_{60-5});
X_3 = apartments as a proportion of the 1960 housing stock (a_{60}/h_{60});
X_4 = proportion of the 1960 housing stock built prior to 1940;
X_5 = percentage of journeys to work made by public transport in 1960;
X_6 = distance of the midpoint of the tract from the Federal Triangle, Washington, D.C.;
X_7 = median family income in 1960.

For the moment it is worth focusing on the first line of the matrix and on the correlations between the independent variables X_3 to X_7. Some of the most interesting and important differences between inner and outer areas can be seen from the latter relationships. They are also shown in Table 9. In the inner area, the highest percentages of old units are found close to the Federal Triangle, but in the outer areas the reverse is true: the average age of the housing stock is greatest in the

		X_1	X_2	X_3	X_4	X_5	X_6	X_7
Growth by apartments	X_1 $\{$ I	1	0.223	0.124	−0.240	−0.121	0.025	−0.095
	O	1	0.483	0.015	−0.018	0.020	−0.057	−0.132
	T	1	0.314	0.027	−0.154	−0.099	0.021	−0.097
Apartment proportion of net growth	X_2 $\{$ I		1	0.425	0.201	0.422	−0.381	−0.591
	O		1	0.437	−0.125	0.396	−0.358	−0.124
	T		1	0.535	0.200	0.511	−0.488	−0.381
1960 apartment proportion	X_3 $\{$ I			1	0.037	0.413	−0.482	−0.340
	O			1	−0.219	0.371	−0.303	−0.266
	T			1	0.140	0.566	−0.500	−0.357
1960 proportion of old units	X_4 $\{$ I				1	0.554	−0.686	−0.200
	O				1	0.142	0.330	−0.143
	T				1	0.576	−0.227	−0.237
Use of public transport	X_5 $\{$ I					1	−0.739	−0.487
	O					1	−0.654	0.112
	T					1	−0.662	−0.358
Distance	X_6 $\{$ I						1	0.367
	O						1	−0.380
	T						1	−0.007
Income	X_7 $\{$ I							1
	O							1
	T							1

I = inner area: D.C., Arlington County, and Alexandria.
O = outer area: Montgomery, Prince Georges, and Fairfax counties.
T = total: inner and outer areas combined.

areas which are still mainly rural. Median income varies in the opposite way, apparently reaching a peak somewhere around the boundaries between inner and outer areas. However, the use of public transport, and presumably its availability, declines continuously and strongly with distance from the city center. One interesting consequence is that, in the outer areas, the proportion of trips to work by public transport is slightly higher in higher income census tracts, reflecting the higher income levels near the District boundary; though in both the inner areas and the whole SMSA, the relationship is quite strongly in the opposite, and expected, direction.

In 1960 the proportion of total housing stock in apartments declined quite sharply with increasing distance from the city center. Although the relationship was not as close as in the inner areas, it was still significant in outer areas. Correspondingly, apartments were most numerous in areas with good transit services. The relationship with income was much weaker, though apparently either poorer families tend to live in apartments, or apartments are built mainly in low-income areas (perhaps because higher-income families could exert more pressure to keep them out), or both.

Table 9. Census Tracts: Washington SMSA Changes with Distance from the Center

Distance from Federal Triangle	1960 census				1960–65			Estimated Jan. 1966 apt. percentage of stock	Number of tracts
	Mean median income	Use of transit	Old units	Apartment proportion	Apts. as percentage of gross additions	Net growth by houses	Growth by apts.		
(1,000 feet)	(...............................*per cent*...........................)								
0– 9.9	$5,058	42.5%	87.4%	63.2%	98.3%	−3.7%	12.0%	69.5%	40
10–19.9	6,960	38.6	61.0	53.5	94.2	−0.8	7.2	57.0	48
20–29.9	8,125	23.2	29.0	43.5	86.4	1.8	14.8	50.1	87
30–39.9	8,708	8.4	21.7	31.0	79.2	6.9	27.1	43.4	67
40–49.9	9,526	6.9	10.2	7.7	41.4	15.9	11.5	15.0	38
50–59.9	8,425	5.0	9.4	3.3	51.3	24.3	25.8	19.4	16
60–69.9	8,442	3.2	13.0	3.3	34.5	51.4	27.0	17.0	12
70–79.9	7,831	3.5	18.1	7.6	26.9	72.2	26.6	17.2	13
80–99.9	6,293	3.1	41.3	10.8	23.3	66.7	20.4	16.6	11
100+	5,892	1.6	49.0	5.1	38.9	23.4	14.9	14.5	13
Total	7,746	21.4	38.2	36.4	60.5	9.8	16.5	41.9	345

Sources: U.S. Bureau of the Census, *1960 Census of Population and Housing,* Series PHC(1). 1960–65 building figures published by individual planning departments and commissions.

From the correlation coefficients in the first line of the matrix one can conclude that the independent variables included fail almost completely to predict where there would be marked growth in the housing stock in the form of apartments in the following six years. For outer areas, none of the coefficients is significant at the 5 per cent level of confidence, though the negative relationship with income comes close. From the over-all data and the data on the inner area it is possible to say that growth by apartments is significantly smaller in areas with a high proportion of old housing. Just those areas which would be expected to be ripe for renewal have been shunned by apartment builders. Once this relationship has been taken into account, the correlation between the residuals and income in the over-all data becomes significant. It enters the regression with a negative coefficient. Again, apartments appear to have been kept out of high income areas. Although these two variables have a significant effect, they only explain 4 per cent of the variation in "growth by apartments." In inner areas, the effect of distance becomes significantly negative. But, again, age of the housing stock and centrality only account for 9 per cent of the variation.

Some difficulties were encountered in using the apartment proportion of total growth as a dependent variable. In any event it was necessary to eliminate all tracts in which there had been no growth during the period. Only a few figures were available for gross additions to the housing stock. However, while gross figures were not available in Alexandria or Fairfax, only gross figures were available for Montgomery and Prince Georges. Although the statisticians at the Park and Planning Commission claim that they can ignore demolitions, since they use the figures mainly for population estimation, it does not follow that they can safely be ignored in this study. In order to try to cover all possible effects, analyses were carried out using (1) the apartment proportion of gross residential building, in which Fairfax and Alexandria were omitted, and (2) the apartment proportion of net growth, in which the assumption was made that demolitions in Montgomery and Prince Georges counties had been negligible. Where net growth is used as the denominator, it is necessary to eliminate all observations for which net growth was equal to or less than zero, even if apartment growth was positive. The resulting negative fraction is not the desired observation. The true value could be infinity but this could not be used either. This resulted in the elimination of thirty observations in the inner and four (all in Fairfax) in the outer area.

The correlations shown in the matrix are for the apartment proportion of net growth. The corresponding values for the apartment proportion of gross growth were always of the same sign and usually somewhat smaller. The most notable difference was that there was no significant correlation between the apartment proportion of gross building and the age of the housing stock. Clearly this is because tracts with the oldest housing had the most demolitions. A very interesting comparison can be made between the second and the third sets of lines in the matrix. There is a great deal of similarity between the relationship of the apartment proportion of net growth to 1960 features of the tract, and of the apartment proportion of the 1960 stock to the same features. In both cases apartments form a higher proportion of total units in low income, close-in areas with good transit services. In both inner areas and over-all the proportion is higher where there are more older units, but in the outer areas the reverse holds.

It would be incorrect to conclude that there has been little change in the location of apartments since 1960. The base of both proportions is total building; up to 1960 in one case, and since 1960 in the other. It is well known that the building of single-family houses during the 1960's has been very much concentrated in the suburban areas, the only areas where there is space to build them. The similarity of the correlation coefficients suggests that apartment building has been migrating to the suburbs as rapidly as house building. There is no obvious reason why it should, because apartment builders can afford to buy old build-

ings for demolition and house builders generally can not. The correla-√
tion coefficient shows the closeness and the direction of the gross relationship but does not show its slope. In fact, Table 9 shows that the
apartment proportion of additions declined less rapidly within a radius
of 11 1/2 miles (60,000 feet), which includes most of the fully urbanized
area. (See Figure 4.)

The change can be seen most easily by using raw figures instead of
the apartment proportion of the stock, and additions to the stock. For
the stock of apartments in 1960, the correlation between number in
any census tract and the distance of that tract from the Federal Triangle
was −0.377, −0.282, and −0.447 for inner, outer, and total observations, respectively. For the apartments built during the period 1960–65,
the correlations were 0.063, −0.096, and −0.004, respectively. In absolute terms, tracts closer to the Federal Triangle did not tend to receive
significantly more apartments during 1960–65 than tracts further away,
though they had very significantly more in 1960. For single-family
houses, the change has been in the same direction, but in this case it
was from a lack of relationship in 1960 to significantly positive in 1960–
65. The relationship with income has changed in a similar way, though

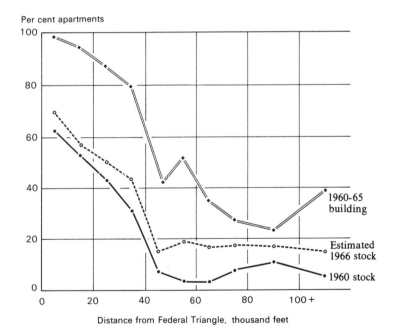

Figure 4. **Apartments as a percentage of total housing by rings: Washington SMSA.**
Sources: See Table 2.

less noticeably. In 1960, tracts with low family incomes contained significantly more apartments. But they did not receive more of the additions.

These changes have occurred throughout the Washington metropolitan area. Although some of the coefficients are different in inner and outer areas, this is at least partly because of the effects of the remote rural tracts. The data have not been arranged to see whether differences in zoning practices produce any of the border effects noted in the previous chapter. For this purpose the outer areas would have had to be analyzed, using distance from the inner area boundary as the distance variable. But the fact that the relationships are similar within inner and outer areas and over the whole SMSA, suggests that "suburbanization" of the apartment market has been a dominant and all-pervading force, and has occurred within the District of Columbia, Arlington, and Alexandria, as well as from them to the surrounding counties.

One of the avowed aims of the zoning of residential land is to separate high-density from low-density uses, on the grounds that high-density are alleged to have undesirable external effects on low-density uses. Census tracts may be too large to use to find out whether this aim has been achieved, but if this aim has a macro dimension—the confinement of high-density housing to a certain section of the county—then tract data can be used. The correlations between X_2 and X_3 are high enough to suggest that there has been some success. Where most of the housing was in the form of apartments in 1960, most of the additional housing has also been apartments, and vice versa. But this gives us little indication of whether there will be more separation than in 1960 or more mixing. Turning again to the raw data, we find that the correlation between the number of apartments and the proportion of apartments in 1960 was 0.811, 0.886, and 0.844, respectively, for inner, outer, and all tracts. In 1960, the largest numbers of apartments were in the tracts with high proportions of apartments to houses. If this extent of separation had been continued during the 1960's, we would expect a continued high correlation between the number of apartments built during the 1960–65 period and the proportion of apartments in 1960, showing that most new apartments had been located in tracts that already contained mostly apartments. But in fact the correlations fall to 0.219, 0.066, and 0.061, respectively. Whatever else we can say about the location of apartments during the 1960's, we cannot claim, except to a moderate extent in the inner areas, that they were close to existing apartment concentrations.

But perhaps the over-all locational shift away from the city center in the demand for apartments made it inevitable that they could not be confined to existing concentrations. A policy which recognized this but wanted to maximize separation would have endeavored to concentrate the additions. There is evidence of some achievement in this direction. Most apartments in the 1960–65 period were built in tracts where they formed a high proportion of net additions ($r = 0.311$, 0.500, and 0.363, respectively), but this represents a much smaller degree of concentration than existed in 1960. It appears on the surface that there was a higher degree of separation in outer than in inner areas. However, this may partly be due to the fact that the rural tracts of the outer areas were not really at risk, and that the inner areas had more tracts which already contained apartment concentrations. It has already been pointed out that a good deal of inner area apartment building had occurred in tracts which did not necessarily receive a high proportion of apartments in their additions. If zoning is regarded as of little importance, or as manipulable, these results might be interpreted as showing that apartments get fewer mutual advantages than they used to from locating close together.

The data were subject to a regression analysis in which only significant independent variables were permitted to enter. This was achieved by specifying a value of the F statistic (in this case 4.0) required before a variable could enter the equation. The resulting regression equations, which might be used to predict the apartment fraction of new housing units, are as follows (standard errors of the coefficients are shown in parentheses).

$$X_2 = 1.093 - 0.00643\,X_7 + 0.322\,X_3 \qquad\qquad R^2 = 0.406 \qquad \text{Inner}$$
$$ (0.00088) \quad\ (0.088)$$

$$X_2 = 0.168 + 0.0204\,X_5 + 0.584\,X_3 \qquad\qquad R^2 = 0.249 \qquad \text{Outer}$$
$$ (0.0057) \quad\ (0.124)$$

$$X_2 = 1.085 - 0.00487\,X_7 + 0.345\,X_3 - 0.00593\,X_6 \quad R^2 = 0.427 \qquad \text{Total}$$
$$ (0.00076) \quad\ (0.078) \quad\ (0.00082)$$

It is significant that a smaller proportion of the variation is explained in outer areas, reflecting the extent to which apartments are a new phenomenon in these areas. The fact that distance from the Federal Triangle enters the third equation and not the others mainly results from its greater variation in the total data. In the other equations the variation associated with distance is represented in the other parameters—to a very large extent by X_3, the apartment proportion of the 1960 housing stock.

Although there is still a significant amount of concentration of apartments, as can be seen from the map of Montgomery County on page 15, the new concentrations have not been closely associated with concentrations which existed in 1960. Frequently they are in small pockets,

Table 10. Building and Rezoning by District: Montgomery County

Area	1960–62			1963–66			Ratio of—		
	Dwelling units built	Capacity rezoned	Capacity rezoned as a proportion of dwelling units built	Dwelling units built	Capacity rezoned	Capacity rezoned as a proportion of dwelling units built	Vacant capacity (1/1/60) and building (1960–62)	Vacant capacity (1/1/63) and building (1963–65)	Vacant capacity (6/1/66) and permits outstanding (6/1/66)
	(dwelling units)			(dwelling units)					
Silver Spring–Takoma Park	3,617	750	0.21	1,905	1,808	0.95	0.86	1.71	6.11
Bethesda–Chevy Chase	865	2,776	3.21	475	2,073	4.36	3.20	12.50	8.41
Kensington–Wheaton	812	369	2.20	442	4,160	9.41	1.22	2.21	6.60
Grosvenor–Twinbrook	170	2,380	14.00	2,842	9,512	3.35	3.84	1.57	5.80
Wheaton–Outer	289	629	2.18	533	8,169	15.33	1.34	1.50	5.94
Potomac	317	0	0	167	1,568	9.39	5.40	8.36	∞
Colesville	0	835	∞	1,525	6,871	4.51	∞	1.27	5.47
Rockville area	0	0	1.00[a]	150	491	3.27	1.00[a]	1.00[a]	∞
Gaithersburg area	0	1,492	∞	340	4,158	12.23	1.00[a]	∞	37.93
Outer county	0	0	1.00[a]	0	445	∞	∞	∞	∞
County Total	6,070	9,231	1.52	8,379	39,255	4.68	1.69	1.90	7.48

∞ Infinity.
[a] Both numerator and denominator are zero.
Source: See Table 7. Data problems are discussed in Chapter 2.

which themselves may be dispersed, or they may be linear concentrations along a highway, or be grouped around an intersection. In any case, it is much less easy to predict where they will occur, using conventional causal factors, than it was to estimate where the existing concentrations were in 1960. The new pockets do not appear to require a high level of transit services, unless their services have expanded more since 1960 than casual observation suggests. Very possibly some of the failures to find significant associations result from the fact that census tracts are too large for the important factors to be picked out. On this level there has been a very considerable spreading out of apartments from their central concentrations. Residential density seems to be the latest way in which the differences between the suburbs and the central city are diminishing.

Table 9 shows changes in housing characteristics from inner to outer rings. Some of the figures from the table are plotted in Figure 4. Apart from the last two rings, each is of equal width and the number of tracts in the inner rings is much greater than that in the outer rings. It is interesting that the dip in the percentage of apartments shown in Figure 4 corresponds to the ring with the highest income level. Both the absolute and the relative increase in the apartment proportion of the total housing stock between 1960 and 1966 were more rapid in outer than in inner areas. Apartment building made its maximum contribution to growth in the housing stock in the rings from about 11 1/2 to 15 miles from the Federal Triangle. For comparison, the maximum contribution made by single-family housing occurred between 13 and 19 miles out, and the two rings of maximum growth overlap to a considerable extent.

The Experience of Montgomery and Fairfax Counties

Has zoning policy had a differential effect between the urban fringe areas and the suburban centers? To examine this question we must compare the rate of rezoning with the rate of building in different parts of the county in order to get some indication of the extent of spare capacity in the inner and outer districts. Table 10 contains information relevant to this. In the first six columns, the rate of rezoning in areas within which Montgomery County has zoning powers (i.e., the whole county except for the Rockville and Gaithersburg incorporated areas) is compared with the rate of building on apartment-zoned land. Although the result is rather uneven, it is clear that Silver Spring–Takoma Park experienced a gradual reduction in the capacity of vacant apartment-zoned land during this period, accompanying the slowdown in the rate of apartment construction. But the other inner area, Bethesda–Chevy Chase, in which there was at least as great a slowdown, had the opposite experience. This resulted from some special factors: (1) A considerable part of the vacant apartment-zoned land is at the extreme north and northwest of the Bethesda–Chevy Chase area, at the fringe of urban development. (2) Rezoning has been the subject of appeals in two large areas. Consequently the capacity of vacant apartment-zoned land actually available for building during much of the period is considerably overstated when additions are dated from the year immediately following the application. (3) Many of the figures are greatly influenced by individual large areas that have been rezoned for apartments during the period.

In the 1963–66 period, rezoning began to run ahead of building much more rapidly in all areas. The exception, Grosvenor–Twinbrook, reflects one large area, Grosvenor Park, which was rezoned in 1960. Building began in 1963, and is still in progress. The greater pace of rezoning, relative to building, is partly a result of the apartment boom itself, and seems to suggest that county councillors expected the rate of building to continue to rise. On the other hand, especially in the inner areas, apartment building on apartment-zoned land might have been slowed down by the large number of units being planned and built in apartment hotels on land zoned for commercial use. This may have reduced the denominator of the equation in an unforeseen way.

In the last three columns of Table 10, the adequacy of the stock of vacant apartment-zoned land at three different dates can be judged by the volume of building in the three years following each of the first two dates, and by the volume of permits outstanding in June 1966 for apartments to be built on apartment-zoned land. A rather different picture emerges here. In particular, there appears to have been considerable surplus capacity in the Bethesda–Chevy Chase and Potomac areas at the two earlier dates. It is worth noting that these were the two major areas in which, the Planning Commission pointed out in 1959, there was too much spare capacity,[10] though the capacity of parts of these areas has since been increased by rezoning to a higher density—from low-density garden to high rise.

One rather unexpected feature is that, in Potomac, Colesville, and Wheaton–Outer, the number of units built between 1963 and 1965, inclusive, was very little less than the capacity of vacant land at the beginning of 1963. Of course, not all the units were built on the land that was vacant at that time. Speculation is sometimes thought of as a process of holding land vacant when conditions are suitable for development. If rezoning had been operating to encourage more of the land speculation–apartment building combination of activities in the outer than

10. Maryland National Capital Park and Planning Commission, *A Preliminary Master Plan of Residential Land Use* (Silver Spring and Riverdale, Md., 1960).

in the inner areas, it might be expected that the average delay from rezoning to building would have been greater in outer areas. There is no evidence of this in Table 10. With the exception of some large areas which have been held for a considerable time in the Bethesda and Potomac districts, the delay appears to be relatively uniform. This test of importance of speculative activity only holds good if speculation, on average, results in an increase in the delay between rezoning and build-ing. But the early part of this chapter showed that the speculative influ-ence on land use decisions does not necessarily involve such delays. So far, then, we can make no clear judgment.

The detailed information about apartments in Montgomery and Fairfax counties can shed some light on the nature and locational characteristics of the suburban apartment boom. First, we are interested in trends over time. The Montgomery County data extend only from 1960 to 1966, plus permits outstanding. The boom had already come to the county by 1960, but it is still true that there have been very substantial changes in the pattern of apartment building during this period. As has already been pointed out, apartments built during 1960 were in similar locations to those built previously. They were similar in other respects as well: all were low- or medium-rise garden apartments built to a density which varied with location—between 14 1/2 and 43 1/2 units per acre—and very few of them could be called luxury apartments.

In some respects the interesting second variable, location, is the basis of the district subdivision of Montgomery County. For the purpose of regression analyses, the distance of each apartment project from the District boundary was used as a continuous variable, although it is neither a satisfactory index of distance from the major suburban commercial centers nor a very good index of travel time to downtown Washington. As already pointed out, urban development has not spread uniformly in all directions from the District boundary. It has generally been concen-trated at the center of the county rather than toward the edges. The western edge especially—along the banks of the Potomac and into the Cabin John watershed—contains a great deal of undeveloped land close to the District. As a result, the "urban fringe" is much closer to the District in those areas than in the Wheaton area. In Fairfax County the distance, for the purpose of regression analyses, was measured from the Federal Triangle in downtown Washington to the center of the census tract in which the apartment was located.

The whole phenomenon of suburban apartments is interesting be-cause it reflects a distortion and perhaps a significant weakening in the relationship between the density of land use and the distance from the city center as postulated in many of the land market models. This may be partly because expressways have made some areas that are distant from the city center quite close in terms of travel time. It will be useful to see whether this distortion has extended to variation in density within a particular land use classification—apartments.

Price theory implies that land values should be an important determinant of density. When the price of land rises, factor proportions will be changed so that less land will be used relative to other factors—labor and capital—and a high density of apartments per acre should result. There are a number of reasons for caution in empirical testing of this relationship. Assessed values (the only land value data used) may not be very accurate when property taxation is based on value of land plus improvements. The important dimension of assessment is the total value of the property. Although assessment ratio studies show that Maryland assessment is of a high standard, it is still possible to doubt the accuracy of the assessed value of land. Property is only reassessed at intervals of about three years and assessments can get seriously out of date in the interim. Finally, once the buildings have been completed, the decision about density is amenable only to very limited variation within a long period. Although it would have been possible to find the assessed value immediately after the apartment project was entered on the Assessor's rolls, this would have involved problems of comparability over time. Even in theory there is no reason to expect a very close relationship between land value and density at a point in time.

In another respect, the relationship between density and assessed value is likely to be too close. It has already been shown that variations in density explain something like 48 per cent of the variations in land value, and I have argued that that is the direction of the causal relationship, at least in this data. The zoning decision is the key which, to a very large extent, determines both density and land values. Apartment builders in most cases build close to the maximum density permitted under the zoning classification. My interest was to determine the extent to which the zoning process was subordinated to, or was susceptible to, pressures from the market. Given that zoning directly determines density, what determines zoning? For these reasons neither the zoning classification, nor the unit value of land, were permitted to enter as independent variables in regression equations to explain variations in density.

In this regression equation the dependent variable was X_1—apartment units per acre—and the independent variables were as follows:

$X_2 =$ the year the apartment came onto the Assessor's rolls, counting 1960 as year 0 and treating permits outstanding as if they were built in 1967;

X_3 = size of project, measured as the number of units in the project which came onto the Assessor's rolls in any one year (this variable understates the size of some large projects built over more than one year), and;

X_4 = the air line distance of the site from the District boundary, in thousands of feet.

The raw data treat as a single observation both the units in each project which come on to the rolls in any one year, and the total number of units (between 2 and 1,100) in any one apartment building permit. But there is an important sense in which the decision to build a large number of units is more significant, in investigating the land market, than the decision to build a small number. For this reason the regression was carried out both with weighted and unweighted data. The weighting system was crude: each observation with between 1 and 100 units was left as a single observation, between 101 and 200 it was duplicated, and so on. The Fairfax County data were not weighted. The permits outstanding were unusual in a number of respects, as discussed on pages 18 and 19. In particular, the apartment hotels were a very special type of development. For this reason the unweighted data has been analyzed with and without permits included. The correlation matrix presents a good deal of data about other relationships (see page 74).

X_5 = plot area in acres;
X_6 = assessed land value per acre;
X_7 = fraction of efficiency and one-bedroom units in total units.

The major conclusion to be drawn is that, with the maximum density limited to rather low levels by zoning regulations, more and more of the apartment building in these two suburban local government areas has taken place at greater distances from the metropolitan center. In Montgomery County this trend would have been reversed if the high-density apartment hotels for which permits were outstanding had actually been completed. Even their completion, since the time of this survey, will not have changed this trend very much. Apartment hotels represent a breakthrough in that they have not been confined within the traditional density limits.

When examining the results in more detail, all but the first group of four lines can initially be ignored. The tendency for density to increase with time is entirely a result of the high density of the projects represented by outstanding permits. Because they are primarily large projects, they have more effect on the weighted data. There has been a slight trend toward lower density in the apartments that have been *completed* since 1960. There is no trend one way or the other in Fairfax County. The relationship between density and size (units in project) also reflects the importance of the large high-density projects among permits out-

			X_1	X_2	X_3	X_4	X_5	X_6	X_7
Density	X_1	WM	1	0.422	0.476	−0.394	−0.395	—	—
		UM	1	0.353	0.464	−0.303	−0.257	—	0.582
		UM-P	1	−0.203	0.122	−0.391	−0.299	0.691	0.457
		F	1	−0.019	−0.186	−0.259	−0.429	—	0.224
Date	X_2	WM		1	0.379	−0.038	0.020	—	—
		UM		1	0.372	0.015	0.157	—	0.435
		UM-P		1	0.137	0.224	0.219	0.385	0.124
		F		1	0.146	0.373	0.013	—	0.070
Units in project	X_3	WM			1	−0.338	0.243	—	—
		UM			1	−0.236	0.451	—	0.410
		UM-P			1	−0.145	0.822	0.018	0.254
		F			1	0.056	0.772	—	−0.126
Distance	X_4	WM				1	0.171	—	—
		UM				1	0.095	—	−0.199
		UM-P				1	−0.007	−0.539	0.085
		F				1	0.197	—	−0.202
Plot area	X_5	WM					1	—	—
		UM					1	—	−0.194
		UM-P					1	−0.282	0.000
		F					1	—	−0.083
Land value	X_6	WM						1	—
		UM						1	—
		UM-P						1	0.115
		F						1	—
Small apartment fraction	X_7	WM							1
		UM							1
		UM-P							1
		F							1

WM = weighted Montgomery data.
UM   = unweighted Montgomery data.
UM-P = unweighted Montgomery data minus permits outstanding.
F   = Fairfax data.

standing. The relationship is, to some extent, spurious in another regard: even though the permit for a large project is taken out at one time, building may take place over a period of years. Hence, there is more disaggregation in the projects completed than in those outstanding. When permits are omitted, the trend to larger size almost disappears. In Fairfax County, where no data on permits were available—all projects were fully amalgamated in the raw data and dated at the time of commencement—there is a slight trend towards smaller projects.

The most important relationship is between density and distance from the District boundary (Montgomery) or the Federal Triangle (Fairfax). Here there is much less variation and in all cases there is less than 1 per cent probability that the value could emerge by chance. These figures all show that density is higher nearer the center of the metropolitan area. In terms of density, at any rate, the traditional highly urban form of apartment still tends to be concentrated in inner areas. However, the correlations are not very high. Less than 16 per cent of the variation in density can be explained by the distance variable. But a good deal more may be explained by other location features which are not included in the regression, such as distance from suburban commercial centers or from major suburban highways. Then, again, apart from the very formal land use models in which there is perfect correlation between density and distance, it is difficult to derive any standard which can be used to judge whether the values of r_{14} are high or low.

The other correlations relating density to plot area, land value, and size of apartment are much as expected. High-density projects tend to be built on smaller than average plots (a capital rationing factor?) and to have a higher than average proportion of small apartment units. The family apartment has always been mainly a low-density building, where children can easily get outside to play.

Distance, date, and units in project have often tended to change together, though not always in the same directions in the different areas and different time spans considered. In particular, there has been a time trend toward larger projects in Montgomery County, mainly as a result of the number of permits outstanding. When these are omitted this trend disappears and Montgomery County behaves more like Fairfax County. The trend away from inner areas is also marked in Fairfax County, and among completed projects in Montgomery County. Correspondingly, the negative relationship between size and distance is very largely produced by permit data in Montgomery County and does not exist in Fairfax County.

As long as Montgomery County did not permit apartments above a limited density, there was bound to be a close relationship between plot area and number of units as builders attempted to build to the maximum permissible density. This relationship has been broken down to a considerable extent in Montgomery by the apartment hotels in the permit data, but it remains very significant even when they are included. Finally, the small apartment unit for single persons and couples without children is becoming more popular in Montgomery, particularly among permits outstanding, and is more common in large projects and where density is high.

The over-all picture is similar for units actually completed in both Montgomery and Fairfax counties. With density fairly strictly curtailed an increasing proportion of new apartments have been built, at somewhat lower densities and with a slightly higher proportion of small units, in outer areas. But the permits in Montgomery County reverse the trend with their high densities, central location, and large numbers of units, a high proportion of which are small. The best fit regression equations are given below, though the coefficients must be interpreted with care, given the high levels of intercorrelation between the independent variables.

Weighted Montgomery County,

$$X_1 = 11.23 + \underset{(2.36)}{18.73}\ X_2 + \underset{(0.0273)}{0.1684}\ X_3 \quad \underset{(0.308)}{-2.351}\ X_4 \quad R^2 = 0.37;$$

unweighted Montgomery County,

$$X_1 = 12.80 + \underset{(2.584)}{10.235}\ X_2 + \underset{(0.0428)}{0.2237}\ X_3 \quad \underset{(0.287)}{-1.156}\ X_4 \quad R^2 = 0.30;$$

unweighted Montgomery County minus permits outstanding,

$$X_1 = 33.77 - \underset{(0.043)}{0.230}\ X_4 \qquad\qquad R^2 = 0.15;$$

Fairfax County,

$$X_1 = 28.01 - \underset{(0.00206)}{0.00544}\ X_4 \qquad\qquad R^2 = 0.07.$$

Table 11. District Comparisons: Montgomery County

District	Mean distance from D.C.	Dwelling units per project	Site area per project	Mean density	Mean land value[a]	Mean % efficiencies + 1-bedroom[b]
	(thousand feet)		*(acres)*		*(dollars)*	
Silver Spring–	3.8	146	2.9	49.8	30,119	63.0
Takoma Park	*4.0*	*116*	*3.2*	*35.8*		
Bethesda–	6.2	236	2.5	95.5	35,250	63.9
Chevy Chase	*6.9*	*112*	*3.4*	*33.2*		
Kensington–	15.1	135	4.1	33.3	23,678	38.6
Wheaton	*15.0*	*112*	*4.3*	*26.0*		
Grosvenor–	30.7	406	16.8	24.4	12,082	38.0
Twinbrook	*30.9*	*405*	*19.9*	*20.3*		
Potomac	28.3	161	11.7	13.8	11,887	24.7
Wheaton–						
Outer	26.7	203	14.0	14.2	13,216	29.2
Colesville	23.6	309	13.8	22.3	17,229	37.2
Rockville	42.6	265	13.5	19.6	17,584	32.0
Gaithersburg	68.1	59	2.8	21.2	11,763	41.9

[a] Excludes projects for which permits are outstanding. Defined as assessed land value per acre.

[b] Sample information only.

Note: Figures in italics exclude, in the relevant districts, apartments built on commercial-zoned land.

Sources: See Table 7.

An alternative way to look at the pattern of apartment building is to examine the features of apartments, district by district (Table 11). To some extent this is another way of looking at the relationship between distance and the other variables. However, as already pointed out, development has not spread from the District of Columbia boundary in an even manner. The districts were described and characterized briefly in Chapter 1; the following should be read in the light of that description. Some time trends can also be usefully examined in this gross fashion (Table 12). They show, for example, the important reversal of

Table 12. Time Trends in Apartment Characteristics: Montgomery and Fairfax Counties

Year and area	Units per project	Site area per project	Mean density[a]	Mean distance from D.C.[b, c]	Mean unit[a, d] land value	Mean % efficiency and 1-bedroom[a, e]
		(acres)	*(units/ acre)*	*(1,000 feet)*	*(dollars/ acre)*	*(per cent)*
Montgomery County						
1960	152	5.8	25.4	14.6	26,960	26.6
1961	166	6.9	28.7	18.2	26,363	24.9
1962	86	3.5	23.9	25.8	23,349	34.9
1963	163	5.7	26.3	25.7	20,873	47.7
1964	120	4.9	22.8	31.5	18,654	46.7
1965	175	8.1	22.4	25.0	13,091	36.2
1966	205	10.9	20.4	33.2	12,063	36.0
Permits	274	4.5	46.4	17.9	—	63.7
outstanding[f]	*179*	*8.7*	*20.2*	*24.4*		*55.4*
Fairfax County						
to 1960	259	13.9	18.7	43.0	—	31.5
1961	249	29.1	8.6	48.3	—	42.3
1962	305	16.3	18.7	47.4	—	54.5
1963	162	8.2	19.6	54.7	—	36.0
1964	156	11.5	13.5	52.1	—	33.5
1965	220	15.8	13.9	52.0	—	39.0
1966	219	29.5	7.4	52.3	—	39.9

[a] Over-all mean for the year; i.e., total units divided by total site area.

[b] Measured from the District boundary for Montgomery County, and from the Federal Triangle for Fairfax County.

[c] Unweighted mean of total projects.

[d] Unavailable for projects at the permit stage.

[e] Includes only a sample of projects for which information is available.

[f] Figures in italics exclude apartments built on commercial-zoned land from permit data.

trend which has occurred in Montgomery County between buildings which were already on the Assessor's rolls in mid-1966 and the permits which were outstanding. Finally, Table 13 shows the trends in density of apartments in each district.

Table 13. Density by Date and District: Montgomery County

District	1960	1961	1962	1963	1964	1965	1966	Permits outstanding[a]
Silver Spring– Takoma Park	26.1	44.7	31.1	48.3	43.6	38.0	38.0	132.1	*44.4*
Bethesda– Chevy Chase	23.0	46.1	43.2	25.7	63.1[b]	54.3	10.5	166.9	*43.2*
Kensington– Wheaton	—	21.8	27.1	21.9	28.3	—	21.8	52.9	*21.6*
Grosvenor– Twinbrook	—	19.5	—	22.0	17.1	22.0	18.9	32.6	*21.7*
Potomac	—	—	18.1	22.1	7.3	—	—	—	
Wheaton– Outer	—	—	16.4	14.4	—	19.3	11.2	13.3	
Colesville	—	—	—	—	20.4	21.2	21.7	23.7	
Rockville	22.2	21.3	19.0	22.1	37.3	—	12.8	14.3	
Gaithersburg	22.7	25.3	25.5	20.7	23.9	12.3	26.7	16.3	

[a] Figures in italics exclude, in the relevant districts, apartments built on commercial-zoned land.
[b] Includes special case.

A problem that arose with the data in their original form was that the measure of project size, taken from the Assessor's rolls, is derived from the number of units that are built in one year in each project. Where projects are built over a number of years the measure underestimates both the number of units and the site value per project. There are also difficulties in amalgamating these observations, because sometimes the zoning (permitted apartments per acre) varies within a "project." It is not always clear whether two groups of apartments should be considered together or not. In the district comparisons shown in Table 11, an attempt has been made to carry out this amalgamation, because in this case dating was not necessary. In the dated comparisons shown in Table 12, amalgamated data have been used in the two columns headed "Units per project" and "Site area per project." Where a project was built over a number of years (some projects had not been completed in mid-1966 and their final size can only be determined from building permits) it was dated in the year when the first units came onto the Assessor's rolls. This has the advantage that the Montgomery County data is comparable with the Fairfax County data, which are dated in this way. It also gives more useful indications of variations in apartment-project size.

In Tables 11 and 13, the districts have been arranged in roughly increasing distance from the District of Columbia boundary. The first two are inner suburban, the next is intermediate, and the following four were all very much outer suburbs in 1960. Gaithersburg is a relatively separate center in the outer county. Rockville is becoming less like Gaithersburg and more like other outer suburban areas with time. It had, both in 1960 and 1966, much more vacant land than Gaithersburg.

Comparing inner with outer suburbs we find most of the differences which would be expected. The differences are more regular and predictable if the apartment hotels are eliminated, but, as I have argued, they cannot be eliminated as uneconomic aberrations of the market. Inner area projects have smaller sites, higher land values per acre, higher densities, and higher proportions of efficiency and one-bedroom units. Each of these differences reflects the fact that apartments in inner areas are more truly urban and cater less for family living and more for single persons and couples without children. It is not easy in inner areas to put together large lots to internalize external land use decisions and hence increase speculative gains. There are no very clear differences in numbers of units per project. Higher densities in inner areas compensate for smaller sites. The Kensington–Wheaton area is intermediate in most respects.

Gaithersburg has small sites, because it is urbanized, but land values are low. The percentage of small apartments is relatively high and densities are higher than would be expected, largely as a result of zoning. The detailed data show a very small variance in densities. The proportion of small apartments is higher than it is in outer suburban areas because the family structure of apartment dwellers in Gaithersburg is much more like a cross section for the whole metropolitan area, whereas the outer suburbs contain a high proportion of the apartment dwellers with families. Rockville has clearly functioned as an outer suburban apartment area for new building in this period.

When the apartments built on land zoned for commercial uses are excluded, most of the differences become less marked. (Since the land value data for apartment hotels has not been included, the unit land value comparisons are unaffected. However, sales of land for apartment hotels are reported at prices of up to $600,000 per acre. With a 60 per cent assessment ratio, assessed values of $300,000 to $400,000 per acre would result.) Differences in density become smaller and the proportion of small apartments no longer varies in any systematic way. On the other hand, differences in site area remain almost unaffected, since it is always difficult to assemble large areas in fully urbanized suburbs. Since density differences are very much muted by zoning restrictions, the number of units per project is now much smaller in inner areas. The developer cannot even get the advantage of large-scale building. Although I have no detailed evidence, it seems clear that the only possible way to develop land profitably in the inner areas as its price rose, when densities could not be increased, was to build increasingly for the high priced market. In both areas there is evidence of an increasing proportion of high-rise buildings at one extreme, and expensive town houses at densities of about twelve to the acre at the other.

The comparisons over time (Table 12) would be expected to show the results of the increased proportion of building that has taken place in outer areas, and its reversal among outstanding permits. There is very little trend in size of project, or of lots, except for a sharp upturn in units per project and a downturn in lot size among the permits, both of which are eliminated if apartment hotels are removed. Without them the mean distance from the District boundary has steadily risen and land values have fallen correspondingly. The proportion of small units has also increased, though irregularly. When apartment hotels are included, the permits outstanding show a spectacular upturn in the proportion of small apartments and in density, and a return to inner locations.

Density and date of building can be seen to interact in Table 13. If apartment hotels are excluded there have been no clear trends toward higher densities among apartments built within one district. One minor exception is Rockville where the city's zoning policy allowed rather higher densities than were permitted in adjacent areas of the county prior to the appearance of apartment hotels. With the increased willingness of the county to rezone land for apartments from the beginning of 1963 onwards, building in Rockville lost something of its attractiveness. The total volume has been small since 1964 and has consisted mainly of town houses.

Apartment hotel densities themselves vary greatly and their influence on the mean densities of all permits also reflects their relative importance among all permits—from something like 87 per cent of all units in the Bethesda–Chevy Chase district down to about 43 per cent in the Grosvenor–Twinbrook district.

High-Rise Building on the Suburban Fringe

One of the most surprising and spectacular features of the suburban apartment boom has been the appearance of apartment towers on the very fringe of urban development. Since 1960 Montgomery County has

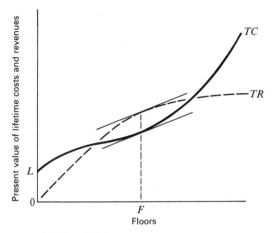

Figure 5. Optimal building height

introduced a high-rise zoning category—R-H. However, it does not permit any higher densities than the maximum of 43 1/2 units per acre
permitted under the old R-10 zoning. It is interesting to ask what in
general determines the optimal height of buildings, in order to see
whether it is possible to shed some light on this phenomenon.

When examining factors affecting decisions about height we will assume here that both the length of life and the time distribution of costs
and revenues are independent of building height. This assumption
makes it possible to deal with the present value of total costs and total
revenues throughout the lives of different buildings without analyzing
differences in their time distribution.

It is quite widely accepted that construction costs per floor are lowest
in buildings of between one and three floors.[11] Total discounted costs
probably follow the same pattern, though in climates where heating
costs are high, two- or three-story buildings may have a greater comparative advantage in total costs than in construction costs alone. Figure 5 plots hypothetical total costs (*TC*) of construction, repairs and
maintenance, and operation, plus cost of land (*OL*) for buildings of
varying height built on a particular plot. Although the general shape
can be drawn with some confidence, the particular shape and position
will vary with the use of the building and construction standards. The
type of building can vary along the length of the curve, though it must

11. P. A. Stone has published results of analyses of effects of building height on
costs; e.g., in "The Economics of Housing and Urban Development," *Journal of the
Royal Statistical Society,* Series A, Vol. 122, Part 4 (1959); and in "The Cost Appraisal
of Housing Developments," *The Building Economist* (Australian), Vol. 2, No. 1 (May
1963), pp. 2–7.

be specified so that the total revenue curve will be for a corresponding
building. Although the curve has been drawn smoothly there are clearly
discontinuities, apart from the obvious one given by the need for the
number of floors to be a whole number. At some stage it is necessary
to install one lift, at another stage, an additional lift. But these discontinuities occur at heights which vary not only with the use to which
the building is being put and the gross area of each floor, but also with
the standard of service that the building provides. Again, as long as the
revenue curve is drawn for the same standard of service at each height,
there is no need to specify any particular rules about the level of service.

A first approximation to the present value of total gross revenue
throughout the life of the building might be a straight line from the
origin, with a slope equal to the present value of rental income per
floor. However, there is a technical reason, given the way the diagram is
drawn, why it should be convex upward. The greater the number of
floors in a building, the greater the proportion of floor space that is
taken up by the service core. If tenants are indifferent to the height of
the floor space they occupy, the total revenue (TR) curve will be convex
upward. It will be even more so if higher floors rent at a discount,
which might easily be true in buildings designed for family-type apartments, or for retailing or service industries that require a good deal of
movement in and out by residents, staff, or customers. On the other
hand, if higher floors rent at a premium because of their view, and
perhaps their prestige, the total revenue curve can straighten and even
become convex downward. The example given by Charles Thomsen[12] for
an office building in downtown Houston estimates a total revenue curve
that is convex downward throughout the range of fifteen to fifty stories.
If the technical factors determining the proportion of usable floor space
in buildings of varying height are taken as given within relatively narrow
ranges, the slope of the total revenue curve over any height range shows
the extent to which the higher floors rent at a premium—or a discount—as compared with the lower floors.

The foremost conclusion to be drawn from this discussion is that the
optimal height of a building is determined—given use, climate, and
other external constraints—not only by the price of land but also by the
positive or negative height premium. The latter factor, which has often
been ignored, is the main explanation for high-rise buildings in areas
of low land value. The effect of a change in the height premium and in

---

12. Thomsen gives a particular calculation of optimal height of a high-rise office
building, which considers revenue as well as cost changes with height; in "How
High to Rise," *American Institute of Architects Journal* (April 1965), reprinted in
The Appraisal Journal, Vol. 34 (October 1965), pp. 585–91.

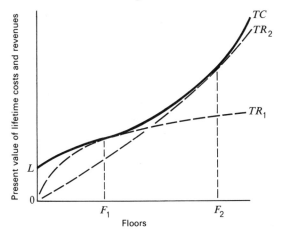

Figure 6. Effect of height premium on optimal height

land value can best be shown by making the competitive assumption that the present value of costs is equal to the present value of revenue at the optimal height, and greater at any other height.[13] The optimal height then becomes the point where TC and TR are tangential rather than parallel as they are in Figure 5.

In Figure 6 the costs remain the same but the height premium is greater in the location or use represented by TR_2 as compared with TR_1. The optimal height will be higher in case 2, even though the average rent per floor is actually lower. If these were two alternative uses on adjacent sites, adjacent buildings of different heights could be explained. In Figure 7 the cost of the site is higher in location 2 but all other costs remain the same. If the revenue is to cover costs it is necessary to find tenants who will pay a higher level of rent in the high land-value location. However, the two TR curves, which have a different over-all slope for this reason, have been drawn with the same (zero) curvature, reflecting a similar height premium. As expected, high land value increases the optimal height of building.

Can it be assumed that there will always be an optimal height for a building? In geometric terms, there will be if the rate of change of the slope of the TR curve, at some height, is less than that of the TC curve. In economic terms, at some stage the rate of increase in total costs from building a further floor is more than the rate at which total revenue increases. Floors of a building cannot be analyzed as if they were homogeneous products. Rent levels can, and often do, vary between floors,

13. This may be because prospective developers bid up the price of land so that all extra-normal profits are passed on to landowners.

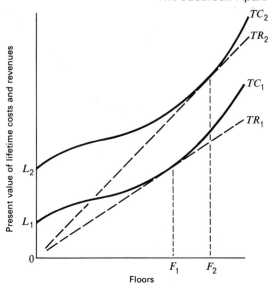

Figure 7. Effect of land price on optimal height

and the type of tenant attracted will also differ. Similarly, two buildings on adjacent lots can opt, rationally, for buildings of different height by aiming at different markets. In one sense they cannot both be right. It would be an unusual coincidence if both made the same net profit, or rate of return. Apart from the fact that owners' discount rates may vary, there is a good deal of ex *ante* uncertainty about the rent-vacancy combinations which are attainable. With a downward convex total revenue curve, the optimal height can vary over wide ranges, depending on the developer's estimates of the values of the key parameters.

Since the land is not expensive, it appears to be the demand rather than the cost side that mainly explains the appearance of high-rise apartment buildings on the urban fringe. For the first time, developers, by taking a risk, have discovered a market on the urban fringe in which tenants are willing to pay very considerable premiums for height.[14]

Because the roof can be developed for a garden and swimming pool, the height premium, or part of it, can be obtained from all tenants. There are very few medium-rise apartments in these areas: most of them are either two- or three-story walk-up garden apartments or structures whose height is limited mainly by local community pressures, building codes or zoning ordinances, or shortages of finance.

14. Leo J. Eikmeyer, in "Analyzing the High Rise Apartment," *The Appraisal Journal*, Vol. 34 (1966), pp. 444–48, quotes a figure of $2.50 per month per floor as the height premium for apartments.

Building height is not necessarily closely related to density. In fact, in outer suburban areas this is unlikely, if for no other reason than that high buildings require a great deal of parking, and this can be most cheaply provided in open car parks. There is no premium for garages with a view, though tenants may be willing to pay something for having their cars stored inside. But very frequently the attraction of the location is partly that the apartment building has a considerable open area around it for outdoor living and recreation. The builders of these apartments have been aiming at a rather special market. Before they built it was difficult to judge how large the market was and at the time of writing there is some evidence in Montgomery County that high-rise apartments have already been overbuilt.

chapter 5

COMPARISONS BETWEEN
METROPOLITAN AREAS

So far, all the detailed information about the apartment boom used in this study has been related to the Washington SMSA, and most of it has been concentrated on Montgomery County within that area. It takes only a very quick glance at the figures to realize that the extent of the apartment boom has varied a great deal between metropolitan areas, despite the fact that its occurrence has been widespread. One would also suspect that the extent of the suburbanization of the new apartment market has varied a good deal. For this reason it was decided to examine some characteristics of forty-one large metropolitan areas for which suitable data were available in order to see what kind of areas had experienced a marked boom in apartments and, particularly, what kind had experienced a boom in the suburbs.

The Data

The U.S. Department of Housing and Urban Development publishes, in its *Housing Statistics,* an annual summary which includes the numbers of building permits issued in certain SMSA's. By supplementing this information with detailed figures published by the U.S. Bureau of the Census in the annual summary volumes of *Construction Reports* (C-40), it was possible, for each of the SMSA's, to separate the numbers of permits issued for the central cities from those issued for the rest of the area for one-family and two-or-more-family structures in each year from 1960 to 1965.

In analyzing these figures I also used statistics of the stock of each kind of housing, and of the proportion of trips to work by public transport in 1960, obtained from the *1960 Census of Population and Housing,* issued by the Bureau of the Census. The main objective was to determine what kinds of cities experienced a high level of apartment building in the first half of the 1960's, especially in suburban areas, and to try to explain some of the variation between metropolitan areas. One other source of data was the Department of Housing and Urban Development's annual *FHA Homes* which contains, for each of the forty-one metropolitan areas, the market price of sites of FHA insured homes. The Federal Housing Administration's Statistical Section supplied me with a new set of data on size of lots in metropolitan areas for 1965, from which an estimate of price per square foot was made. Since the series does not go back to 1960, estimates of unit land value in that year were made on the assumption that there had been no change in lot size between 1960 and 1965. Since these data are used only in comparative analyses of the forty-one SMSA's, all that really matters is the assumption that there has been no change in relative size of lot.

There are a number of data problems. The only detailed housing unit statistics which are published for metropolitan areas are for building permits. But a building permit is only followed by construction after a variable delay, and sometimes not at all. This is especially important in the case of apartments, where the average delay is probably longer, and the possibiltiy that an apartment will never be built is greater. The delay is also more variable because builders apply for large numbers of permits when market expectations are high but may delay building for some time if the market becomes sluggish. Permits taken out at the peak of the boom are also most likely to be allowed to lapse. A favorable change in rezoning policy may make sites available which previously could not be used for apartments, and this can stimulate a considerable amount of permit activity in a short time, though the buildings may be constructed over a very much longer period.[1] An even more marked bunching of permits may occur if developers expect an unfavorable change in rezoning policy in the future, and rush to obtain permits before it occurs. House building is less subject to periodic overbuilding followed by shortages and these fluctuations are not nearly as marked.

The unit land price data are mainly collected in suburban areas. They do not reflect in any way the price which apartment builders have to pay. Rather they indicate a part of the opportunity cost of living in apartments. If land for single-family housing is expensive, apartments become a relatively more attractive alternative. Analysts with a good deal of experience in the urban land market have argued that the FHA values are reasonably accurate as indicators of market price.[2]

Table 14 shows apartments as a percentage of all housing stock in each of the forty-one large SMSA's, both at the time of the 1960 Census and (from building permits issued) during the period from 1960 to 1965. The same information is shown for the parts of the SMSA's which lie outside their central cities. The relative increase in the percentage of

1. According to Louis Winnick, this is the main explanation for the 1961 and 1962 boom in numbers of apartment permits in New York: "Rental Housing: Problems for Private Investment," *Conference on Savings and Residential Finance* (Chicago: U.S. Savings and Loan League, 1963), pp. 101–12.
2. For example, see Sherman Maisel, "Price Movements of Building Sites in the United States—A Comparison of Metropolitan Areas," *Regional Science Association Papers*, Vol. 12 (1964), pp. 47–60.

Table 14. Significance of Apartments[a] in Forty-one SMSA's

SMSA	Total SMSA			SMSA outside central city		
	1960 Census % apartments	1960–65 permits % apartments	Col. (2) ÷ col. (1)	1960 Census % apartments	1960–65 permits % apartments	Col. (5) ÷ col. (4)
	(1)	(2)	(3)	(4)	(5)	(6)
Atlanta	26.2%	44.8%	1.71%	11.2%	29.7%	2.64%
Baltimore	21.6	46.2	2.14	11.6	29.1	2.51
Birmingham	16.3	20.8	1.27	5.2	8.6	1.66
Boston	52.7	53.5	1.02	39.9	40.3	1.01
Buffalo	43.7	23.4	0.53	22.4	20.1	0.90
Chicago	53.7	49.0	0.91	19.2	37.6	1.96
Cincinnati	43.2	45.0	1.04	23.8	18.2	0.76
Cleveland	37.1	52.3	1.41	17.4	48.1	2.76
Columbus	24.7	36.0	1.45	7.3	19.6	2.68
Dallas	18.0	44.6	2.48	6.6	28.7	4.34
Dayton	16.3	30.9	1.89	9.1	17.3	1.90
Denver	25.2	37.6	1.49	13.2	23.9	1.80
Detroit	24.5	27.5	1.12	10.3	22.7	2.21
Fort Worth	12.5	27.7	2.21	3.4	20.0	5.84
Houston	16.0	56.9	3.57	2.9	35.3	12.09
Indianapolis	20.5	37.7	1.84	3.4	32.8	9.62
Jacksonville	16.5	23.1	1.40	4.6	20.4	4.43
Kansas City	26.2	33.3	1.27	10.6	28.5	2.69
Los Angeles–Long Beach	28.3	61.9	2.19	18.4	54.9	2.99
Louisville	21.4	24.7	1.15	4.8	15.0	3.09

Memphis	19.4	40.1	2.06	3.4	9.3	2.77
Miami	33.4	59.0	1.76	25.5	51.4	2.02
Milwaukee	43.7	53.4	1.22	19.4	31.2	1.60
Minneapolis–St. Paul	31.4	50.3	1.60	7.0	35.1	5.03
New Orleans	40.4	43.2	1.07	10.9	31.4	2.89
New York	71.2	69.4	0.97	23.2	25.3	1.09
Orlando	12.7	18.9	1.48	6.1	13.7	2.26
Philadelphia	19.0	49.6	2.61	11.9	43.3	3.64
Phoenix	12.0	39.0	3.26	10.2	26.9	2.64
Pittsburgh	23.5	27.9	1.19	16.2	17.6	1.09
Sacramento	18.6	42.0	2.26	8.6	41.2	4.78
St. Louis	32.0	38.5	1.20	10.4	32.1	3.08
San Bernardino–Ontario–Riverside	8.9	33.8	3.79	6.8	30.1	4.44
San Diego	21.2	38.7	1.82	11.3	34.8	3.09
San Francisco–Oakland	36.1	57.2	1.59	17.3	49.2	2.84
San Jose	15.6	48.0	3.08	11.7	58.0	4.94
Santa Barbara	17.3	42.1	2.43	12.4	35.2	2.85
Seattle	23.4	28.8	1.23	7.2	13.6	1.88
Tampa–St. Petersburg	15.2	16.2	1.07	8.4	12.3	1.47
Tucson (Arizona)	9.5	41.0	4.33	4.2	19.8	4.68
Washington, D.C.	40.6	65.3	1.61	26.4	60.2	2.28

[a] Apartments in 1960 data are defined as all structures containing more than one housing unit; i.e., by Census definition. This excludes one-family attached houses. Apartments in 1960–65 data include row houses.
Sources: U.S. Bureau of the Census, *1960 Census of Housing,* HC(2); U.S. Department of Housing and Urban Development, *Housing Statistics, Annual Data;* U.S. Bureau of the Census, *Annual Construction Reports* (C40).

apartments is shown by comparing additions with stocks. The table indicates that the boom was geographically widespread, at least among metropolitan areas, and that the suburban areas of most SMSA's experienced a more marked upsurge in apartment construction than did their central cities. The strength of the boom in suburban apartments varied a good deal. Some of the smaller areas, like Cincinnati and Buffalo, continued the trends of the 1950's, with an increased proportion of single-family houses in the suburban housing stock. In other areas, such as San Francisco and Washington, there was a very large reversal of this trend.

Although the Census differentiates between one-family attached houses (duplexes and row houses) and apartments, the permit figures do not. The extent of the apartment boom is, therefore, probably exaggerated in Table 14 because attached single-family houses are counted as one-family units in columns (1) and (4), and because, in the new housing market, garden apartments are, in many respects, playing the role formerly played by row houses. Consistency would have been best served by including one-family attached houses with apartments in columns (1) and (4), but apartments and row houses are very different. Moreover, it is unlikely that a large number of row houses have been built since 1960. (In 1960 they comprised 2 per cent of multiple-family housing in Montgomery County, Maryland.)

Although it is not shown in Table 14, there was also a great deal of variation in the timing of the boom. In Denver the proportion, and number, of apartments reached its peak in 1961; in New York, in 1962; and in most of the California metropolitan areas, in 1963. On the other hand, 1965 found the number and proportion of apartments still rising in Washington, Detroit, Miami, and Philadelphia. There is some evidence of a cycle which occurs at different times in different areas. After a spurt, apartment building slackens off considerably, while single-family house construction maintains a relatively fixed level. Chicago is one outstanding exception. There, the numbers of permits for both types of units have remained remarkably constant throughout the first half of the 1960's.

The Building Cycle Hypothesis

One explanation for the occurrence of the apartment boom, as noted in Chapter 2, is that it succeeded a boom in office construction. When, in the late 1950's and early 1960's, it became evident that the supply of office accommodation exceeded the level of demand, many builders had spare capacity admirably suited to building apartments. The cyclical explanation can help to account for the timing of the upsurge, but if it is the main, or only, explanation, we would expect the boom to be followed by a downturn. The concept of a cycle in apartment construction that is little related to the building of single-family houses is illustrated in Figure 8, which shows the numbers of permits issued for selected metropolitan areas during the first half of the present decade. Though often less marked, this pattern is repeated for most of the forty-one SMSA's.

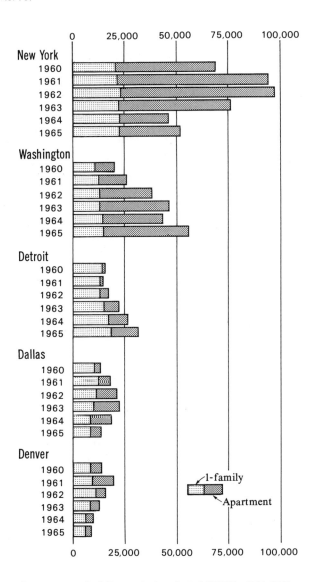

Figure 8. The apartment building cycle in selected SMSA's, 1960–1965

If cycles are important in apartment building, but not in house building, the proportion of apartments among total permits will be high in
years in which the total number of permits issued for housing unit construction is also high. In Table 15, the values of the coefficients of
correlation between the apartment proportion of permits and the total
number of permits issued in a given year is shown for the forty-one
SMSA's used in this study. In itself, this is a test of whether apartment
construction fluctuates more than house building. But given observations like Figure 8, it does provide some test of the existence of a cycle.
A high positive correlation shows that in years in which the numbers
of permits issued was high, apartments formed a high proportion of
those permits. Although the series is so short (six years, 1960 through
1965) that only very high correlations have, by themselves, statistical
significance (roughly half the SMSA's have values of r significant at the
5 per cent level); the fact that the values of r are so concentrated near
1.00 reinforces the significance of the individual observations.

**Table 15.   Correlation between Percentage of Apartments and Total Number of
Permits Issued in Forty-one SMSA's**

Value of r	No. of SMSA's	Mean 1960 housing units	Value of r	No. of SMSA's	Mean 1960 housing units
		(thousand)			*(thousand)*
0.90 to 1.00	15	606	−0.09 to 0.00	0	—
0.80 to 0.89	6	723	−0.19 to −0.10	2	276
0.70 to 0.79	7	622	−0.29 to −0.20	0	—
0.60 to 0.69	2	255	−0.39 to −0.30	1	107
0.50 to 0.59	2	478	−0.49 to −0.40	0	—
0.40 to 0.49	1	85	−0.59 to −0.50	1	57
0.30 to 0.39	1	620	−0.69 to −0.60	1	141
0.20 to 0.29	0	—	−0.79 to −0.70	1	301
0.10 to 0.19	1	1,997	−0.89 to −0.80	0	—
0.00 to 0.09	0	—	−1.00 to −0.90	0	—
	35	627		6	193
			Total or mean	41	563

The second point to note is that the exceptions are found mainly
among the smaller SMSA's. The 68 per cent (by number) of the SMSA's
that had correlations between 0.70 and 1.00 contained 77 per cent of
the total housing units in 1960. The most important exception is Chicago
($r = 0.11$), which shows very little evidence of any fluctuations in apartment construction during the first half of the 1960's.

It would be helpful if we could look at each SMSA throughout a full
cycle and see whether the proportion of apartments after the completion of the cycle was greater or smaller than before its commencement.

Unfortunately the statistical series are too short to do this. In all, except New York, of the SMSA's that appear to have completed, or nearly completed, their cycles, apartments comprised a higher proportion of permits issued in 1965 than they did of the total stock of housing in 1960. New York is unusual in a number of respects, not least in the importance of rent control. The SMSA comprises a central city plus only some of its suburbs, mainly the more affluent ones. New York City and the suburbs separately had a slightly higher proportion of apartments in 1965, and in that year building in the city was very slack. Louis Winnick, writing in 1963, said that overbuilding had been stimulated in New York by a favorable new zoning law, and predicted the fall in the next two years.[3]

Perhaps, then, there is something more than a cycle to explain which, even if it has been part of a cycle, has been important enough to significantly change the composition of the stock of housing. In the Washington SMSA the number of apartment permits issued in the six years, 1960 through 1965, was equal to some 65 per cent of the apartments existing at the 1960 Census.

The Extent of the Apartment Boom

It is possible to test some of the hypotheses about apartment development by looking at the experience of different metropolitan areas in the first half of the 1960's and comparing this with the composition of the stock of housing at the time of the 1960 Census. Since all of the variables used are continuous, they have been analyzed by using stepwise regression, choosing a small number of independent variables. A by-product of the program is a complete matrix of simple correlation coefficients, and a listing of the partial coefficients between the remaining independent variables and the dependent variable, as each successive independent variable is introduced into the regression. In defining variables used in the regression analysis the following symbols, comparable to those used in Chapter 4, will be used:

$$H = \text{SMSA total housing units;}$$
$$HS = \text{suburban total housing units;}$$
$$A = \text{SMSA total apartments;}$$
$$AS = \text{suburban total apartments;}$$
$$\text{Subscript } 60 = \text{1960 Census stock;}$$
$$\text{Subscript } 60\text{–}5 = \text{permits issued during those years.}$$

$X_1 = $ proportion of apartments in housing permits issued for the SMSA, 1960–65 $= A_{60\text{–}5}/H_{60\text{–}5}$;
$X_2 = $ proportion of apartments in total housing stock, 1960 $= A_{60}/H_{60}$;
$X_3 = $ relative increase in the proportion of apartments, i.e.

3. Winnick, *op. cit.*

$$X_1/X_2 = \frac{A_{60-5}/H_{60-5}}{A_{60}/H_{60}} \ ;$$

X_4 = mean of 1960 and 1965 site values in dollars per square foot;
X_5 = relative increase in site values, i.e., 1965 price/1960 price;[4]
X_6 = percentage of journeys to work made by public transport in 1960;
X_7 = rate of growth (construction), i.e., total 1960–65 housing unit permits/
      1960 stock = H_{60-5}/H_{60} ;
X_8 = SMSA size as indicated by total 1960 housing units (in millions)
      = $H_{60}/10^6$.

A matrix of simple correlation coefficients follows.

	X_1	X_2	X_3	X_4	X_5	X_6	X_7	X_8
X_1	1.000	0.552	0.136	0.320	0.136	0.482	0.168	0.519
X_2		1.000	−0.616	0.172	−0.231	0.832	−0.418	0.637
X_3			1.000	0.050	0.474	−0.500	0.601	−0.225
X_4				1.000	0.050	−0.080	0.339	0.102
X_5					1.000	−0.194	0.374	−0.042
X_6						1.000	−0.512	0.676
X_7							1.000	−0.293
X_8								1.000

The great problem with any statistical analysis of this data is the high correlation between what are supposed to be independent variables. Perhaps the most important is that $r_{68} = 0.676$, which makes it almost impossible to separate the effects of SMSA size and transit use. Both, of course, to some extent reflect pressure on the land market. However, there are large SMSA's with very poor transit services and it might have been expected that a good transit system would lend itself to the development of apartments. SMSA size reflects, among other things, the length of the journey to work. One would expect that in large SMSA's the alternative to living in apartments relatively accessible to workplaces is much less attractive, because journeys to work are longer than in smaller cities. The median size of lots of FHA-insured homes was inserted as an independent variable in some of the regressions. However, it is closely related to land values ($r = -0.698$) and its effect on the various dependent variables was always less than, and swamped by, the effect of land value. Where land value had no significant effect, neither did lot size.

Variations in the proportion of apartments, 1960–65 (X_1).   In this regression analysis, the most obvious result was that large SMSA's with good transit services had a high proportion of apartments among the permits issued in the first half of the 1960's. The same SMSA's had a high pro-

4. As noted on p. 87, the unit prices of sites were estimated on the assumption that there was no change in relative lot size between SMSA's between 1960 and 1965 as lot size information is available only for 1965.

portion of apartments in the 1960 stock. The main complicating factor was the cyclical element in apartment building which increased the proportion of apartments among SMSA's whose stock of buildings grew rapidly during the period.

The independent variables X_4 through X_8 were tested to see whether they could assist in explaining variations in X_1. The program used was similar to that used in the analyses reported in Chapter 4. It did not force any of the independent variables into the regression, but permitted the computer to select successively variables which, when included in the regression, produced the greatest reduction in the residual variance. It did not permit variables to enter unless they contributed significantly to the goodness of fit of the regression. Because of the intercorrelation among the independent variables, the regression equations are probably of less interest than the sign and size of the simple and partial correlation coefficients and the value of R^2, which shows the fraction of the variation in the dependent variable which can be explained by the independent variables. The simple correlation coefficient matrix suggests that it should be possible to explain a high proportion of the variation in X_1. All the variables are included in this matrix. In some respects, relations between the independent variables are as interesting as those between dependent and independent variables in shedding light on the nature of the apartment boom.

It appears that either SMSA size, transit rating, or the character of the city housing market (as expressed in the 1960 proportion of apartments in total stock) would be a relatively good predictor of the 1960–65 proportion of apartments. The higher the price of land, the greater the proportion of apartments. The apartment proportion also increases with both SMSA size and the availability of transit. Both SMSA size and transit rating are more closely related to the proportion of apartments in 1960 than to the proportion among permits issued between 1960 and 1965, but the opposite is true of land price. Rapidly growing SMSA's had a slightly higher proportion of apartments in 1960–65, but those with a high proportion in 1960 grew much more slowly during this period. This latter is related to the fact that larger SMSA's grew more slowly ($r_{78} = -.293$) and that the older cities in the eastern states, in which the 1960 proportion of apartments was higher, grew more slowly than the younger, lower-density SMSA's in the West. What appears to emerge from the simple correlation coefficients is that there is a group of large cities with good transit which are characteristically apartment cities. They also tend to have high land prices, at least in the suburbs.

One figure that does not conform with this picture is the positive, though low, correlation between rate of growth and the apartment proportion of permits. When the effect of SMSA size is taken out, the correlation becomes very much stronger ($r_{17.8} = 0.391$). When, in addition, the effect of the use of public transport is taken into account, the relationship becomes stronger still and the rate of construction enters the regression equation and becomes the most significant independent variable. The explanation for this behavior can be found in the cyclical pattern of apartment growth discussed earlier in the chapter. SMSA's which have experienced a full cycle of apartment growth during 1960–65 tend to have both a higher rate of growth and a higher proportion of apartments than those which, like Denver, were close to the peak in 1960, or, like Detroit, did not get underway until some time during the period.

A significant part of the association between the 1960–65 and the 1960 proportions is accounted for by their common association with these three variables ($r_{12.678} = 0.326$). However, there are still some special features of cities—probably age and location—which are reflected in the 1960 proportion but not in any of the other independent variables. The "increase in land price" variable, X_5, does not have a significant relationship with X_1 and the relationship does not become more significant as the effects of the other independent variables are entered into the regression. Perhaps rapidly rising prices make apartment as well as house ownership more attractive, and increasing land prices can force an increasing number of people out of the house market and into the apartment market. The dangers of generalizing from a cross sectional relationship to a time series relationship are underlined in a case like this. Higher land prices in some cities can stimulate apartment building because a more land-intensive kind of accommodation is costly, but rapidly rising land prices have a great deal to do with the attractiveness of ownership.

The regression equation of best fit was as follows:

$$X_1 = -0.875 + 0.0077\ X_6 + 0.678\ X_7 + 0.058\ X_8 \qquad R^2 = 0.514$$
$$(0.0024) \qquad (0.168) \qquad (0.030)$$

The standard errors of the coefficients are shown in parentheses. The coefficient of X_8 is significant at the 5 per cent level and the others at the 1 per cent level. The two largest SMSA's, New York and Los Angeles–Long Beach, fit the regression poorly. Surprisingly, perhaps, New York had too few apartments during 1960–65 and Los Angeles–Long Beach too many.

Variations in the relative increase in the proportion of apartments after 1960. The apartment boom is measured by the ratio of X_1/X_2—i.e., X_3—which was taken as the dependent variable in the regression analysis.

The major conclusion is that the boom has been strongest in the SMSA's which had a small proportion of apartments in 1960 ($r_{23} = -0.616$) so that it has increased the similarity of the composition of the housing stock in different SMSA's. SMSA size, land prices, and transit availability have become dramatically less important since 1960, indicating that the apartment boom does not appear to be a response to the disadvantages of life on the expanding urban fringe.

In this analysis it seemed useful to add the 1960 proportion of apartments, X_2, to the list of independent variables as it is not clear, a priori, whether the boom in apartments would be expected to occur mainly in cities which already had a high proportion of apartments, or whether it was an opportunity for those with relatively few apartments in 1960 to catch up some of their lost ground. The table of simple correlation coefficients points strongly to the latter. The apartment boom, as I have defined it, is stronger in small SMSA's despite the fact that large SMSA's had a higher proportion of apartments in the 1960 stock and among the 1960–65 permits. Apparently the boom has been strongest in SMSA's with the poorest transit services ($r_{36} = -0.5$). That rapidly growing SMSA's experienced a strong apartment boom is highlighted by the correlation of 0.6 between X_3 and X_7.

When the "catching-up effect" is removed by entering the 1960 proportion into the regression, the correlation between the residual variation in X_3 and rate of growth remains high at 0.480. However, the effect of the use of public transport apparently cannot be separated from the effect of the 1960 proportion of apartments ($r_{63.2} = 0.028$). There is certainly no evidence here that a good transit service was necessary to experience a large increase in the proportion of apartments, though high absolute percentages of apartments still occur where the service is adequate. This is, though, much less true of permits issued since 1960 than it was of housing built prior to 1960.

Although the absolute level of land value is not significantly related to the extent of the apartment boom, it does appear to have stimulated (or have been a consequence of) high increases in land values ($r_{35} = 0.474$). Land values have risen more rapidly in the fastest growing cities, but those which experienced a large apartment boom appear to have been particularly strongly affected. This may indicate either that apartment developers were attracted by the possibility of speculative gain, or that their operations tended to raise the price of lots for house building. It also shows that if house builders are strongly attracted by the possibility of speculative gains, the implied relationship between house building and land value increases is swamped by other influences. After removal of the effects of construction rate and the 1960 proportion of

apartments, the correlation between SMSA size and the residual variation in X_3 actually reverses from -0.225 to 0.336 and just fails to enter
the regression positively. When other significant factors have been taken
into account, then, the apartment boom has been stronger in larger
SMSA's.[5] The regression equation, with standard deviations in parentheses, is:

$$X_3 = -1.787 - 2.611\ X_2 + 2.689\ X_7 + 0.866\ X_5 \qquad R^2 = 0.578$$
$$(0.736) \quad\ (1.005) \quad\ (0.395)$$

Each of the coefficients is significant at the 1 per cent level. In this case,
the equation predicts relatively well for the larger SMSA's, though New
York, Los Angeles–Long Beach, and Chicago all had somewhat larger
apartment booms in the 1960's than would have been expected from
the equation. This result shows again how strongly the "catching up"
phenomenon influences the regression.

Although apartments have continued to be concentrated in large
SMSA's with good public transport services, this was dramatically less
true in the first half of the 1960's than it was prior to 1960. Most of the
independent variables which are inserted to see whether the pressure of
high land prices or different urban facilities can account for differences
in the strength of the apartment boom either have a weak effect, like
SMSA size; no independent effect, like transit use; or no observable
effect at all, like land price. This seems to suggest quite strongly that the
apartment boom of the 1960's has not resulted from increasing pressure
of higher land prices and longer journeys to work. Such a pressure can
be met most satisfactorily by living in an apartment where a good transit
system permits journeys to work that are shorter than travelling by automobile from a single-family house at the fringe. In fact it seems that the
strongest factors are either demand influences—such as taste or demographic changes—or supply changes which are somewhat independent
of those characteristics of cities reflected in the independent variables
used in the regression. Hence the strength of the catching-up phenomenon. Although regional customs and public transport availability are still
important in determining the composition of additions to the housing
stock, they are much less important than they used to be.

I have suggested that the close associaton of the rate of growth with
the extent of the apartment boom is partly a reflection of the cycles of
apartment building and of the timing of the construction boom in various SMSA's relative to the period for which the statistics have been
assembled. It also happens that the SMSA's which grew more rapidly

---

5. The last step in the regression analysis was to enter X_5. The difference between
$r_{35.27}$ and $r_{38.27}$ was very small. Either one, entering the regression, would have
reduced the power of the other to explain the remaining residuals to just below the
significant level.

tended to have a smaller proportion of apartments in 1960 and therefore had to do a considerable amount of catching up ($r_{27} = -0.418$). However, it is at least possible that this association could reflect to some extent the problem that rapidly growing SMSA's might face if the house building industry had limited capacity for expansion. The only way to meet an upsurge in housing demand might be by building apartments. However, the house building industry was able to meet similar increases in demand in the 1950's, and its national rate of production actually declined after 1959.

A good public transport system has not been a necessary condition for a strong upsurge in apartment building in the early 1960's. However, at least some of the apartments could have been built with the expectation of better public transport becoming available to serve them in the future. Washington and San Francisco have both experienced strong increases in numbers of apartments during this period and both have relatively well advanced plans for developing their transit systems. In any case, the figures on the use of public transport are for 1960 and do not reflect the extensions of service or of use that the apartment boom may have occasioned since then. (However, a very high proportion of apartments built in suburban Washington appears to be automobile oriented.) The extent to which the apartment boom has been concentrated in the suburbs (analyzed in the next section) throws further doubt on the importance of this factor.

The Suburban Apartment Boom

In some of the SMSA's shown in Table 14, there has not even been a statistical increase in suburban apartments since 1960 that could be called a boom. In others, the increase has been so small that it could easily have been caused by a spillover of central land uses. One problem encountered in interpreting the figures is that in different SMSA's the central city takes up different proportions of the total area and stock of housing. If the central area spillover accounted for a large part of the increase in suburban apartment building, it would probably be greatest in SMSA's where the central city (statistically) is a small part of the total metropolitan area. Table 16 shows the percentage of housing units and apartments which were outside each central city in 1960. In that year, there was a higher proportion of apartments than single-family houses inside the central city in each of the forty-one SMSA's. In forty of these SMSA's, the 1960–65 additions reduced the concentration of apartments in the central cities; in twenty-four of them, a smaller proportion of the apartment permits issued during 1960–65, than of the total stock of housing units in 1960, were concentrated in central cities.

Table 16. The Changing Role of the Suburbs in the Housing Market

(Per cent)

SMSA	Units outside central city as a percentage of all SMSA units			
	All units 1960	All units 1960–65	Apartments 1960	Apartments 1960–65
Atlanta	50.0%	68.0%	21.5%	45.1%
Baltimore	44.2	70.8	23.7	44.6
Birmingham	44.0	66.2	13.9	27.3
Boston	70.7	73.1	53.5	55.1
Buffalo	56.7	93.5	29.1	80.3
Chicago	39.2	69.6	14.0	53.4
Cincinnati	50.1	60.7	27.6	24.5
Cleveland	49.7	84.8	23.4	78.0
Columbus	29.0	36.8	8.6	20.1
Dallas	36.2	46.4	13.3	29.8
Dayton	60.6	80.3	33.9	45.1
Denver	43.3	73.3	22.8	47.0
Detroit	52.0	90.1	21.8	74.4
Fort Worth	35.7	60.2	9.8	43.5
Houston	23.3	12.5	4.3	7.8
Indianapolis	29.0	62.7	4.8	54.4
Jacksonville	52.2	90.2	14.6	79.7
Kansas City	49.7	68.2	20.1	58.2
Los Angeles–Long Beach	54.9	67.3	35.7	59.6
Louisville	42.7	72.8	9.7	44.2
Memphis	17.8	47.5	3.1	11.1
Miami	65.6	80.8	50.0	70.4
Milwaukee	35.6	50.8	15.8	29.9
Minneapolis–St. Paul	40.5	71.4	9.0	49.9
New Orleans	25.4	65.0	6.8	47.3
New York	24.3	34.8	7.9	12.7
Orlando	71.1	87.0	33.4	61.6
Philadelphia	51.3	67.0	32.2	58.5
Phoenix	32.5	55.6	27.6	39.2
Pittsburgh	73.5	81.7	50.6	51.5
Sacramento	56.4	79.5	26.1	77.9
St. Louis	60.2	88.2	19.6	73.5
San Bernardino–Ontario–Riverside	75.3	83.7	57.3	74.6
San Diego	43.4	53.2	23.0	47.8
San Francisco–Oakland	53.8	78.6	25.8	67.6
San Jose	65.5	53.7	49.3	64.9
Santa Barbara	60.4	79.7	43.2	66.7
Seattle	45.0	73.0	13.9	34.6
Tampa–St. Petersburg	41.5	69.0	22.9	52.7
Tucson (Arizona)	19.0	53.5	8.5	25.8
Washington, D.C.	57.6	85.2	37.5	78.6

Sources: U.S. Bureau of the Census, 1960 Census of Housing and annual Construction Reports.

Six new variables were defined for the purpose of analyzing the suburban apartment boom. Each of the independent variables used previously in this chapter to examine apartment growth by SMSA's was retained. The new variables are as follows:

X_9 = proportion of apartments in housing permits issued outside the SMSA's central city, 1960–65 = AS_{60-5}/HS_{60-5} ;

X_{10} = proportion of apartments in total housing stock outside the central city, 1960 = AS_{60}/HS_{60} ;

X_{11} = relative increase in suburban apartments, i.e., X_9/X_{10}

$$= \frac{AS_{60-5}/HS_{60-5}}{AS_{60}/HS_{60}} ;$$

X_{12} = proportion of the total housing stock found inside the central city in 1960

$$= \frac{(H-HS)_{60}}{H_{60}} ;$$

X_{13} = proportion of apartments found outside the central city in 1960
$= AS_{60}/A_{60}$;

X_{14} = relative increase in the suburban share of SMSA apartments, i.e., suburban share in 1960–65 permits/$X_{13} = \dfrac{AS_{60-5}/A_{60-5}}{AS_{60}/A_{60}}$

The matrix of simple correlation coefficients shown below excludes those already shown in the previous chapter. There are some gaps where the relationships between variables are not interesting.

	X_9	X_{10}	X_{11}	X_{12}	X_{13}	X_{14}
X_4	0.538	0.267	−0.053	−0.116	0.244	−0.026
X_5	0.115	−0.157	0.172	−0.049	0.117	−0.115
X_6	0.106	0.493	−0.308	0.234	−0.220	0.055
X_7	0.360	−0.193	0.263	−0.101	0.272	−0.160
X_8	0.260	0.426	−0.213	0.067	−0.017	−0.138
X_9	1.000	0.464	—	−0.293	—	—
X_{10}		1.000	−0.534	−0.388	—	—
X_{11}			1.000	0.325	—	—
X_{12}				1.000	−0.875	0.399
X_{13}					1.000	−0.562
X_{14}						1.000

Variations in the proportion of apartments in the suburbs. The first regression analysis took X_9 as the dependent variable and permitted X_4 through X_8 and X_{12} to enter as independent variables. The major conclusion was that high suburban land prices were the most important explanatory variable, but that SMSA's with more apartments in their suburbs in 1960 continued to receive more among new housing. It is interesting to note how much weaker is the association of use of public transport and SMSA size with the 1960–65 proportion of apartments in the suburbs, than with the 1960–65 proportion in the SMSA. On the other hand, high land values are associated more with a high proportion of apartments in suburban permits than with a high proportion in total SMSA permits. Of course, the land value data (from the Federal Housing Administration) are predominantly for suburban land, so it is not surprising that their effect was felt more strongly in the suburbs than in the central cities.

Land value is, in fact, the only variable to enter significantly into the regression to explain the proportion of apartments in suburban permits. When this variable has been entered, the ability of other independent variables to explain variations in the residuals is not significant. The nearest is growth rate ($r_{97.4} = 0.224$ whereas r_{97} is 0.360). Land values are highest in rapidly growing cities, and part of their apparent influence may be due to their correlation with growth rate (and vice versa for the equations in the previous chapter, where growth rate entered as an independent variable but land value did not). The partials for both relative size of the central city and SMSA size are somewhat smaller than the simple correlations.

The predicting equation shown below does not explain much of the variation in the dependent variable. It is significant that, unlike the results of the SMSA analysis, the fairly genuinely independent variables are not able to explain the variation which, in gross terms, is associated with the features of the 1960 stock of housing ($r_{9\ 10.4}$ is 0.395, not very far below the simple $r_{9\ 10}$ of 0.464). Although it remains well below the level of significance, the partial correlation between the proportion of suburban apartments and the use of public transport rises when the effect of land value is taken out. When the composition of the 1960 suburban stock (X_{10}) was permitted to enter one experimental regression, the value of R^2 was very much higher (0.500), and the rate of growth actually entered the equation as well. When each of the variables (X_4, X_7, and X_{12}) had entered the equation, the partial correlation of transit use with the dependent variable was even higher, though still not significant at the 5 per cent confidence level. The regression equation of best fit is

$$X_9 = -0.891 + 0.256\ X_4 \hspace{3cm} R^2 = 0.290$$
$$(0.064)$$

Apartments have played a relatively important part among the additions to the housing stocks in the suburbs of SMSA's where they were already important in 1960, and have been much more important where the price of suburban land for housing is high. SMSA size, the availability of public transport, and rate of growth all appear to have had less influence on the composition of additions to the suburban housing stock than to the SMSA stock, though rate of growth and land price are too closely related for their influence to be completely separate.

Variations in the relative increase of suburban apartments. The next regression took X_{11} as the dependent variable. In this way, the procedure adopted for the SMSA's was used for the suburbs: first, the actual proportion of apartments among permits, and then the ratio between it and the proportion of apartments in the 1960 stock were examined. In effect, I looked first at the composition of marginal additions to the housing stock and then at the marginal-average relationship to see at what rate the average composition was changing. In this respect, X_{11} is comparable to X_3.

The independent variables which were admitted to this regression analysis were X_4 to X_8, X_{10}, and X_{12}. Among these, by far the best explanation of variations in the extent of the apartment boom in the suburbs is given by variations in X_{10}: the smaller the proportion of apartments among the suburban housing stock in 1960, the greater the relative increase in that proportion in 1960–65 ($r_{10\ 11} = -0.534$). Again the catching-up effect dominates the regression. In different SMSA's the housing stocks in the suburbs—as in the whole SMSA—are becoming more alike in composition. Once the effect of this factor is taken out of the variations in X_{11}, no other independent variable has a significant correlation with it. In this respect it is interesting to compare the simple correlations shown in the matrix with the partial coefficient, once the catching-up effect has been removed.

| | | Correlation with extent of the suburban apartment boom, X_{11} | |
		Simple (r_{i11})	Partial ($r_{i11.10}$)
X_4	Land value	−0.053	0.109
X_5	Rise in land value	0.172	0.106
X_6	Use of public transport	−0.308	−0.061
X_7	Rate of growth	0.263	0.192
X_0	SMSA size	−0.213	0.019
X_{12}	Proportion of SMSA housing in central city	0.325	0.151

It appears that, to a very considerable extent, the suburban apartment boom was most notable in SMSA's which had poor transit services, were relatively small, and had relatively large (statistically) central cities, because these SMSA's had a small proportion of apartments in 1960. This can be confirmed by examining the simple correlation between these variables and X_{10} in the matrix. The positive simple and partial correlation coefficients of X_{11} with X_{12} imply that the apartment boom, as defined in X_{11}, becomes stronger farther from the central city. We cannot have too much confidence in the other values shown above, though they generally confirm other evidence about the nature of the boom; e.g., both high and rapidly increasing land values are associated with a large suburban apartment boom, as is a high rate of growth of the housing stock of the SMSA.

The regression equation of best fit is

$$X_{11} = 4.96 - 14.72\ X_{10} \qquad\qquad\qquad R^2 = 0.28$$
$$(3.73)$$

Variations in the relative increase of the proportion of SMSA apartments in the suburbs.   The final regression took X_{14} as the dependent variable and X_4 to X_8, X_{12}, and X_{13} as the independent variables. Even though the suburban apartment boom is expressed here in rather different dimensions, it is still dominated by the trend for SMSA's to become more alike ($r_{13\ 14} = -0.562$). The regression including the only variable with a coefficient significantly different from zero is

$$X_{14} = 4.52 - 7.37\ X_{13} \qquad\qquad\qquad R^2 = 0.32$$
$$(1.74)$$

The simple correlation coefficient shows that SMSA's with a high proportion of total housing stock in central cities experienced a large increase in the proportion of apartments located outside the central cities. But the high negative correlation between X_{12} and X_{13} (-0.875) indicates that it is not possible to separate the catching-up effect, shown by the relationship between X_{13} and X_{14}, and the rapid increase in the proportion of apartments found in the suburbs in those SMSA's which had relatively unimportant suburbs in 1960; i.e., where the proportion of housing in the suburbs increased substantially, so did the proportion of apartments. This is further evidence that the boom has been greater in the outer suburbs. If one assumes that the central city occupies the innermost and highest density part of the SMSA, only the outer suburbs are counted as suburbs at all in SMSA's dominated, statistically, by their central cities. Of course, $r_{9\ 12}$ (-0.293) suggests that the proportion of apartments among permits is still lower in the outer than the inner suburbs.

chapter 6

LAND USE DECISIONS
AND IMPERFECTIONS
IN THE LAND MARKET

The Development-Redevelopment Decision

A good deal of urban land use theory has been based on long-run models which assume that the use of land adapts completely to current circumstances. But this kind of adjustment can only occur after a period long enough to permit replacement of all obsolete buildings and other capital structures. When it is remembered that roads and streets are a part of the land use pattern and that they have a particularly strong effect on other land uses, it can be seen that the long run is very long indeed. Many of the capital structures which are built on land, after a decision has been made about its use, are long lived, relatively specialized to that use, and difficult if not impossible to move to another site.

However, many of the problems of urban land use are partly caused by the durability, inflexibility, and immobility of improvements to the land. It seems to me that a good deal more attention should be paid to short-run use in an effort to discover when it would be profitable to change the use to which a plot of land is devoted.

The land use decision is an investment decision that has a number of peculiar qualities. In the first place, the value of the land itself—which reflects the discounted value of the flow of net returns from the most profitable alternative use of the land—can change over time. If the short-run land use decision is dominated by this factor, as it may be on the urban fringe, changing it could be compared to making a decision to sell maturing wine or maturing forest trees for timber. If there is no income from land being held vacant on the urban fringe the situations are very similar. The return from postponing the development decision is the increase in the value of the land, less any holding costs, such as property taxes and maintenance charges, T. The value of land for development at any time, t, is the present value, at that time, of the flow of future net returns, positive and negative, that can be expected if it is decided to develop at that time. Hence, the returns to an owner from postponement from t to $t + 1$ are $(PV_{t+1} - PV_t) - T$. The cost to him of postponing is either the interest he could get if he sold the land for development, $i.PV_t$, or the cost of waiting one period (year) before he starts the cycle of investment and returns which, at the time it starts, will be worth PV_t. This, again, is equal to $i.PV_t$.[1]

As long as the expected increase in the value of the land, less taxes, exceeds the opportunity cost of holding it vacant, it will pay to postpone development. There may, in fact, be a number of different kinds of bidders in the market, some of whom intend immediate development, while others, who might be called speculators, specialize in holding vacant land while it matures for development. If they bid against each other for the land, its price will be equal to the present value of the returns when redevelopment is planned for the best time; i.e., the time which will maximize present value. In a cost versus returns sense can say that development will take place when

$$(PV_{t+1} - PV_t) - T = i.PV_t . \tag{1}$$

This equation will give us a sensible result if we regard the PV's as relating to development at the time nominated. But if we regard them as actual land prices, then, in a perfect land market, the equation will always hold for vacant land because speculators will always bid up the price of land until it is just far enough below the expected price next year to cover taxes and the costs of waiting. Of course, the land market is not perfect but the active presence in it of bidders who are willing to hold land vacant makes it more nearly perfect.

One of the important qualifications to this analysis relates to the uncertainty of the future returns. Generally speaking, our knowledge about the future is smaller the more distant the time period concerned. Hence it is useful to use the concept of "discounting for uncertainty." Conventional discounting takes account of the fact that returns received in the future are of less value to us than returns received currently because of what we could do with the money in the interim. Discounting for uncertainty takes account of the fact that expected returns in the future are less valuable than those received currently because we are much less sure how large they will be; a bird in the hand is worth two in the bush.

In most instances there will be some current revenue from the use to which land is committed, even if it is only used for agriculture. The situation on the urban fringe, where changes in land values dominate

---

1. Assuming that interest is payable at the end of each year, the cost of postponing will actually be $\dfrac{i.PV_t}{1+i}$ if he sells and takes the interest, and $PV_t - \dfrac{PV_t}{1+i}$, which is equal to $\dfrac{i.PV_t}{1+i}$, if he waits a year to start the cycle. The assumption that it is paid at the end of the year will also be used, with perhaps less reality, in the case of rent receipts. It does not affect the argument in principle.

the decision making, can be compared with that in a stable residential area, where land values do not change very much. In the latter circumstances, buildings are quite similar to other kinds of capital investment and all that need be said is that they are replaced when they wear out or become obsolete. If the buildings are regarded as investments and are producing rental income, we can expect that the net rental income, after repairs and maintenance, management, and other operating expenses have been met, will decline with the age of the building. On the one hand, rental revenue will tend to fall because of increasing obsolescence, and, on the other, repairs and maintenance will become more expensive as more components of the building reach the end of their maintenance-free life.

The costs of postponing redevelopment are the same as the costs of postponing development of vacant land, namely $i.PV_t$. But in a stable area the returns from postponement are the net revenue being earned from the current development on the land (i.e., net of property taxes as well as operating costs). Let us call the revenue net of operating costs in time period t, R_t. Then we can say that redevelopment will become profitable when R_t falls so that

$$R_t - T = i.PV_t. \qquad (2)$$

PV_t refers, of course, to the most profitable type of future use for the land. As long as the left-hand side of the equation exceeds the right it will pay to postpone redevelopment. This analysis can be applied to owner-occupied housing, though it becomes necessary either to talk of the satisfaction it provides to the occupants, or the imputed rental value of their living accommodation, instead of R_t.

In order to produce a general set of rules for changes in land use which involve changes in the structures on the land, it is necessary to amalgamate these two elements and to take account of the fact that land values can fall as well as rise. The general formula for the conditions when a change in land use is profitable becomes

$$R_t + (PV_{t+1} - PV_t) - T = i.PV_t \qquad (3)$$

It has been suggested earlier that in a stable area R_t will generally tend to fall as the building ages, but in an area where land values are increasing, R_t can increase continuously and disguise increasing obsolescence and running costs. However, redevelopment will still become profitable if PV_t rises sufficiently rapidly that the opportunity cost of postponing the receipt of the increased revenue actually overtakes the net revenue in its present use. This is probably the pattern of events leading to redevelopment in the centers of many large cities.

The opposite extreme occurs in areas where the old and obsolete buildings are falling in value. Although their net rentals may actually be declining, the value of land and buildings in the area may also be declining; consequently the revenue that could be expected from a single new building may decline as rapidly or more rapidly and redevelopment may never become profitable. In this extreme case there is a kind of negative speculative effect because the expression in parentheses on the left side of equation (3) actually has a negative net value.

Of course, redevelopment will not occur just because land values are increasing in an area. If land devoted to its present use yields net returns which increase as rapidly as those available after redevelopment, there will be no incentive to change the use. One suspects that this may be true in many of the slum areas where the rents that can be obtained from accommodating those who, because of limited income, have a high demand for slum housing, can increase quite rapidly.

So far it has been assumed that the factors determining the value of the land for development or redevelopment at any particular time are outside the control of the owner. This is probably a fair assumption in the case of the small landowner, since the value of land, or of a particular development on a plot of land, is determined largely by the uses of other land in the vicinity. However, the large-scale landowner and developer can internalize these external effects and ensure that the uses of his land are located in such a way that their complementarity and the value of his land are maximized.

Apart from the general problem of making decisions under conditions of uncertainty, all the decisions described so far have been consistent with the use of land for the purpose which is best from the point of view of the community as well as of the individual owner. This applies as much to the decision to withhold land from development as to the decision to develop or to redevelop. If the present value of the flow of returns from land which is unused for ten years and then used for apartments exceeds that which would result if it were used for single-family houses now, it is in the community interest that it should be held vacant for ten years (unless there is some useful interim use). The value of the activities of speculators applies particularly to the owner of a large lot who increases its value by ensuring complementary uses of its various parts. The result is co-ordination of the kind that planners strive to achieve. This also applies to the owner who increases the value of his own land by ensuring, by some means, that other land in the vicinity is used for purposes that complement the use to which his own is put.

Market Imperfections and Their Effects

The analysis developed in the first part of this chapter can be used to determine whether a number of the alleged imperfections of the urban land market are likely to have any effects on the allocation of land to apartments. In this chapter, imperfections present in the market itself and in other related markets are considered, ignoring, as far as possible, the public sector. In Chapter 7, imperfections are examined which result from non-optimal public policy and are specifically related to the public sector of the urban economy.

Land speculation. Land speculation has two positive roles: (1) the promotion of an optimal timing of land use changes and (2) the encouragement of landowners both to enlarge their activities to provide complementary land uses, and to induce owners of other land to engage in complementary activities. These roles have been defended as generally improving resource allocation. Critics of the market often condemn speculation, pointing to the margin between agricultural value plus costs of urban servicing on the one hand, and price of sites to the builder on the other. It is time to examine this more closely and to determine how an over-all acceptance of the role of land speculators should be qualified.

By land speculation is usually meant the use of land for something other than that which would bring the highest current net returns (e.g., holding it vacant), in the hope that future developments will more than compensate for the loss in current revenue by a higher future sales price or flow of returns. There are two distinct functions here which should be separated for the purpose of analysis, even though any land speculator will perform both in unknown proportions. One would occur even if the future were known with certainty; namely, holding land for development later at a positive cost, as analyzed in the previous section. The other is uncertainty bearing, a kind of insurance function. These two functions can be separated in principle but not in practice because the value of almost every plot of land can be expected to change in a way that will affect land use decisions at some time, and the expected future value is always uncertain. A similar situation prevails in the commodity market: whenever commodities are stored their value changes in an uncertain way. In both markets there are owners who are mainly interested in the expected gain in values, and others who are mainly interested in bearing uncertainty in return for an expected positive net revenue.

A third motive, essentially nonspeculative but not always easily separated from speculative uses, for owning land or commodities is for their current use. Consider a farmer on the urban fringe who holds land while the fairly predictable spread of urban development increases its value for housing, and who sells it for single-family housing. His is mainly a holding function, though he can never be certain when a developer will buy his land. But the same farmer who holds land while single-family housing is built all round him, in the hope that he can sell it at a much higher price for a shopping center, is more an uncertainty bearer. The non-speculative owner is typified by the house owner, though, as is suggested in Chapter 2, even he has not been oblivious to capital gains. In the commodity market, for instance, storage between harvests mainly performs the withholding function, while storage of, say, metals in the hope of a price rise is more uncertainty bearing. The nonspeculative owner needs the commodity as part of a normal inventory. In many commodity markets the two functions can be very largely separated through the use of the futures market. A good deal of the risk can be avoided, at a fairly predictable cost, by hedging. There is no such alternative in the land market, though an owner can develop part of his land and hold the rest for later development.

Let us first ignore uncertainty to explore the implications of land holding speculation a little further. On the urban fringe, as soon as the present value of the expected increase in returns from urban uses becomes significant, the value of agricultural land increases beyond the present value of the expected returns from agriculture. At this stage, the increase in land value appears to have little economic function, except to dissuade the farmer from investing in long-term land improvements for agriculture. But in a situation of no uncertainty it does not distort land use either. Profits (including capital gains) are maximized by keeping the land in agriculture. When the time comes to change the land use, the kinds of considerations discussed in the previous section will become relevant and the bidder who takes into account changes in expected future returns will reflect the true current value of the land in his bid. The land use which maximizes the present value of future returns is, in fact, the best. One way to look at this function is to see how it regulates the rate of development on the urban fringe. If only current returns were considered in bidding for land, the result would be rather curious. All land on the fringe would first be built at a very low density. Many of these buildings would soon have to be demolished to make way for successively higher-density buildings; clearly a very wasteful procedure.

Land speculation is often blamed for increasing the price of suburban land. Speculators enter the market and bid against those who want the land for current use. The contrary argument is that land only has a value in use, and speculators can only bid up to that value, discounted to the present. However, this argument assumes that the price paid for land for current use is independent of supply conditions. If speculators become more active in the market, future uses will bid more actively against current uses. The price can be forced up because the demand for land for current development will be somewhat lower if the price is higher. When speculators enter the market the supply curve of land available for current development is shifted to the left. When speculation is becoming more active the price of land will rise more rapidly but, once speculation has reached a given level of activity, it will release some land to, and withdraw other from, development and need not affect the rate of change of prices. At the present level of analysis one can only say that the more active speculation is, the better the timing of land use changes will be.

Does this activity result in land prices that are too high? They will only be above their true value to the community if (1) the discount rate of speculators is lower than the social rate, as, for example, it may be in underdeveloped countries, or (2) for some other reason those holding vacant land do not pay the full cost of holding it. These questions will be considered later in this and the next two chapters. In general, the intertemporal pattern of land use changes will be better when land uses which represent different time patterns of investment and net returns can compete actively.

Uncertainty introduces a number of complications which are probably best treated separately. (The effects of the imperfections which uncertainty introduces into the capital market will be treated on pp. 113–18.) Some uncertainty can be avoided by encouraging favorable uses of nearby land. When the future use of land on the urban fringe is uncertain we normally say that future returns are discounted for uncertainty as well as futurity, so that the price of land tends to be below the present value of expected future returns. The margin will vary between bidders, depending on the extent of their aversion to uncertainty, so that the land will frequently fall into the hands of those who do not have a strong aversion to risks—often people who have high incomes. There are, however, other reasons why land speculation is a game for the wealthy, as will be shown later.

Because landowners differ in their evaluation of expected returns from different uses in the future, and because they put varying rates of discount on uncertainty, there is a good deal of leapfrogging in urban development. In a world with no uncertainty or in a highly planned world, land would only be withheld from single-family housing when it was cheaper to hold it vacant for later use—for shopping centers, apartments, schools, etc.—than to build and later demolish houses. But, because of uncertainty, considerably more or (less frequently) less land may be held out of the initial phase of development.[2] Leapfrogging, or what Jack Lessinger has called "scatteration,"[3] can occur when no one is certain where a particular shopping center will be located. Lessinger defends this type of development as being less likely to be allowed to deteriorate and less inhibited by neighborhood effects. For instance, if a group of old houses which are ready for development is not too large, it will not cause a neighborhood as a whole to deteriorate at the rate of the individual houses, and consequently the returns from development will not be depressed (i.e., $i.PV_t$ will be maintained as R_t falls). It will be possible to renovate and redevelop in manageable portions and the externalities which usually retard redevelopment will become less important. This gain from speculation is a windfall, since discount rates are high enough for the planning horizon of developers to be shorter than the expected life of the buildings.

Compared with a planned world in which the future is known with certainty, uncertainty always results in the misallocation of resources. Too much land will be held out of current development here, and too little there, producing vacant lots, scattered development, and wasteful demolition of valuable buildings. One advantage claimed for scattered development is that it produces vacant lots, which can play an important current role in providing informal and free recreation areas for children. On the other hand, of course, land can also be used for purposes which turn out to be less than optimal, although it is wrong to blame land speculation for the misallocation of land which results from the existence of uncertainty. It can easily be argued that, given this uncertainty, land speculation helps us to make the best of the situation. Much talent and effort is devoted to making the best estimate of future conditions. One of the important functions of planning is the reduction of the extent of uncertainty, and the consequent improvement of resource allocation. Speculators can do this themselves, too, but only very imperfectly.

One particular effect of uncertainty is that land which is being held mainly for speculative motives often remains unused. In part, this is because the owner wants to be in a position to realize gain from sale at very short notice. Even farming the land, or leasing it to a tenant, ties it for some time and makes it a less liquid asset. In addition, those

2. More land is usually withheld than is used because the gains from possible high-density uses are great enough that the probability of use does not need to be very high. Moreover, the losses from a bad guess may be quite low since accessible land is more valuable, even for single-family houses.

3. Jack Lessinger, "The Case for Scatteration: Some Reflections on the National Capital Regional Plan for the Year 2000," *Journal of the American Institute of Planners*, Vol. 28 (1962), pp. 156–69.

skilled at judging future trends in land use and values are, not surprisingly, often without farming experience, and approaching urban development has adverse effects on the productivity of the land for agriculture (picnics, children, stray dogs, etc.).

As long as there is uncertainty, and as long as the timing and even the co-ordination of urban development is largely carried out in the private land market, it does not make sense to decry the role of land speculators. Their role would become less important and less profitable if there was more certainty about future urban developments. In the next section, and in Chapter 8, it will be argued that imperfections in the capital market and some bad governmental policies make speculation too profitable. The verdict thus far must be that it is not harmful and that speculators do, in fact, play a valuable role in any largely unplanned land market.

Imperfections of the capital market.[4] Capital is allocated most productively when the rate of return at the margin is the same in all uses. This will occur in a private market if the cost of capital is the same in all uses and to all users, and all of the other usual conditions hold. The cost of capital can vary from one user to another because of the costs of borrowing and lending, and because security is required for loans. Thus, the person with little security quickly reaches the maximum he can borrow. To devote more capital to buying land, he has to sacrifice some other use of his scarce funds and their value in this alternative use (the opportunity cost) may be very high. By contrast, a lender, who may pay high income tax rates, is willing to use capital to get even a very low rate of return or satisfaction, especially if it is tax free. The opportunity cost of capital is the value of having $1 this year, over and above the value of getting it one year hence. Users with a high opportunity cost could use their capital very productively during the year and therefore the cost of waiting (discount rate) is high too: it equals the opportunity cost of capital. The user with a higher opportunity cost of capital (generally a borrower) will be forced to restrict his spending in areas where there is a long wait for returns relative to areas which produce immediate income or satisfaction. Conversely, the person with a low opportunity cost of capital (generally a lender and/or a landlord) will be able to afford to bid up to a high price for assets with a long life because he discounts future returns at a low rate. It would normally be expected that those with a low rate of discount would specialize in productive

4. For a very informative discussion of this problem see M. Mason Gaffney, "The Unwieldy Time-Dimension of Space," *The American Journal of Economics and Sociology,* Vol. 20 (1961), pp. 465–81.

processes with a long production period; conversely, those with a high discount rate would prefer processes with a short production period. Where the assets are required for consumption (e.g., housing), or where production requires a combination of assets and other inputs, the factor market permits the "lender" to hire the labor and skills of the "borrower" or to lend capital or lease assets, including land, to him.

However, transactions in the factor market are not costless, particularly when the value of the factor itself is to some extent at risk as its flows of services are used. In the case of labor, the problem is not very important as there is relatively little risk to the factor itself and that risk is insurable. But with both capital and land there is a substantial and uninsurable risk that part of the value can be lost in the process of production, or as their flows of services are consumed. This risk is uninsurable because it depends partly on the skill of borrower or leasee and cannot be assessed actuarially. The margin between borrowing and lending rates of interest is partly due to the kind of uncertainty that was discussed in the previous section. This is particularly true as far as the real estate market is concerned. Land and buildings would be very much better security for borrowing if future changes in urban areas could be forecast with more certainty. Differences in discount rates are, in the first instance, due to differences in wealth and skills and to progressive income taxes. But, if the costs of administration of loans and leases were zero, these differences would be ironed out by transactions in the real estate and capital markets. All of these features can be regarded as integral parts of the capitalist system and to complain that they misallocate resources is much like saying that too many Cadillacs are produced because their buyers really have a low marginal utility of money. Both complaints are more closely related to the equity of the economic system than to its efficiency.

If the margin between discount rates can be reduced by planning, tax policy, or credit policy, it is useful to look at its effects. Because, for all practical purposes, land lasts forever, it has the longest average period between investment and returns of any asset; i.e., there is a very long waiting period, on average, between buying the asset and obtaining the income or satisfaction from it. In fact, the price covers a flow of returns assumed, usually, to last forever, and often to increase with time. By contrast, most other assets depreciate and give off fewer services as they age. Hence the capital cost of land is higher than other assets relative to net annual returns; e.g., with a twenty-year life, an asset returns $(i + 0.05)K$ where i is the going rate of return and K is capital value of the asset. Capital is recovered in twenty years. But, with land, returns are iK (assuming a static situation) and the capital cost can only be recovered by sale. As a consequence, the bids of buyers with a low opportunity cost of capital, who discount returns in the distant future less strongly, tend to be higher for land, relative to other bids, than for other assets.[5] Buildings also rank high on capital cost/annual returns rates as most of them have a useful life of at least thirty to forty years. Land, in particular, and buildings to a lesser extent, tend to be owned mainly by those with a low opportunity cost of capital, and rented to those with a higher opportunity cost/discount rate.

Under these circumstances there are two alternatives for the borrower who needs accommodation. He can either borrow on the security of buildings and land, or he can rent. Sherman Maisel[6] lists a number of alternative forms of borrowing, each of which differs in the difficulty and cost to the mortgagee of getting title to the real estate in the event of default. The lender demands better security; i.e., a higher proportion of the value of the asset has to be "deposited," if he is to take the risk of costly resumption. Tenancy comes at one end of this list, requires a very small deposit, and the title does not change hands. Eviction is sometimes difficult, but this is clearly the best alternative for a "borrower" for whom the opportunity cost of capital is very high. At the other end comes the ordinary mortgage.

One reason for the transaction cost of borrowing real assets (leasing) is the cost of supervising the lease and ensuring that the value of the security is maintained. Supervision costs so much more for single-family than for multiple-family housing that very few single-family houses are built for rental purposes. Many, of course, are rented when the owner moves away for short or long periods, but the closest thing to houses built for renting is the town house which has characteristics somewhere between a detached single-family house and an apartment. Problems are also involved in the separate ownership of multiple-family housing. Co-operatives and condominiums cannot entirely eliminate the frictions which result from common ownership of parts of the building, and the need to take joint decisions and assume joint responsibility.

Anything that increases tenancies is likely to increase the volume of multiple-family housing and anything that increases ownership is likely to increase the demand for single-family houses. If, by more generous credit or by improving knowledge about future urban development, credit were to become more readily available, ownership would become

5. A good deal of this analysis derives directly from M. Mason Gaffney, *op. cit.*; "Land and Rent in Welfare Economics," in Joseph Ackerman, Marion Clawson, and Marshall Harris (eds.), *Land Economics Research* (Resources for the Future, 1962); and "Ground Rent and the Allocation of Land among Firms," in *Rent Theory, Problems and Practices*, Research Bulletin 810 (University of Missouri, North Central Regional Research Publication No. 139, 1962).
6. Sherman Maisel, *Financing Real Estate* (McGraw-Hill, 1965), Chapter 1.

more common and rental housing less popular. However, this would mainly affect cheaper apartments because if families can afford to live in high-income apartments they can generally afford to buy if they want to. Hence, the cheaper suburban apartments, the older downtown apartments, and converted houses would suffer. With less demand for rental housing in inner areas, there would be a stimulus to redevelopment and, if tenants were able to buy their houses, there would probably be more renovation. This might, of course, be offset by a lower demand for moderate or low-income apartments.

In the first part of this chapter, it was assumed that the same discount rate was used to discount future net revenues to find their present value and to find the cost of delays; i.e., the income that could be earned if the capital invested in the land was freed by selling it, and invested elsewhere. I have already suggested that land ownership will be especially attractive to investors with a low discount rate. But after development it might be sold to, say, house owners and the value of the land might be determined by the value that such "borrowers" place on the net returns available over time, discounted at their higher rate. However, the costs of withholding it from development are borne by a "lender" with a low rate of discount.

If there is some rate at which the community as a whole discounts future returns and that rate is between the discount rate of the owner of undeveloped land and the owner after development, redevelopment will be delayed longer than is socially desirable. This can be seen most clearly by using equation (1), though it also holds in the redevelopment decisions characterized in equation (3). Let C represent the costs of withholding land from current development in equation (1), p. 106 (i.e., $i.PV_t$) and N the returns from withholding ($PV_{t+1} - PV_t$) when both are discounted at the community rate, say 6 per cent. Now, as the final user requires a mortgage and has an opportunity cost of capital of 8 per cent, the present value of the land at all time periods will be equal to 6/8 of its value at a 6 per cent discount rate to him, and hence on the market in the developed state.[7] Both PV_t and N, the returns from withholding land from development, will be reduced by the same factor, 0.75. But the cost of waiting is borne by the low-discount-rate landowner, for whom i is less than 6 per cent, say 4 per cent. Hence C', the cost actually borne will be $C\dfrac{4}{6} \cdot \dfrac{6}{8} = 0.5C$. His returns, as noted above, will be $0.75N$. If this is a typical pre- and post-development situation, it follows that the returns from withholding land from devel-

---

7. This follows from the fact that land gives off an infinite stream of returns and, if they are uniform, the present value is R_t/i, where R_t is the annual net return and i is the rate of discount.

opment or redevelopment have been increased, as compared with the situation where all discount rates are the same, relative to the costs. It follows that the imperfection of the capital market discussed in this section is likely to lead to undesirably delayed development and redevelopment, and a parallel undesirable stimulus to land-withholding speculation. If this analysis is correct, it could justify policies which reduce the margins between the opportunity cost of capital to "borrowers" and "lenders," or ameliorate its effects on land use.

The above example best fits the case of development for single-family housing where the value of land varies closely with the discount rate of the typical single-family house buyer, who is generally a borrower. But rental housing values are affected by the discount rates of property owners, which are likely to be closer to those of the landowner or developer. For the tenant, rental housing has a negligible waiting period.

One of the least satisfactory results of the distribution of buying power which results from relatively free pricing of goods and productive factors is that the purchase of a house, a basic need, requires a considerable accumulation of wealth. It is composed of two of the longest lived of all assets. The private lending and leasing markets can offset these problems to a considerable extent, though both are costly to operate. The governments of many countries have assisted in house purchase by providing, subsidizing, or insuring credit for house purchasers. Other attempts to solve some of the problems have been made by the use of rent control, public provision of low cost housing, urban renewal policies, and housing codes. One important purpose of all of these policies is to permit poor families to occupy better housing than, with their income and wealth, the private market will provide. Another implicit purpose is to permit families, who would otherwise only be able to rent, to own houses. There appears to be a value judgment that ownership of a single-family house is the right of all families who have a moderate income.

Government finance or guarantees have often been a major stimulant to speculation. In terms of our model, they increase the bids for the current use of land (for low income housing) and so increase the cost of holding land off the market. But an almost automatic concurrent effect is to raise $(PV_{t+1} - PV_t)$. If redeveloped housing is to be stimulated, it will also be necessary for policies to be aimed at reducing the current rentals obtainable from deteriorated housing by reducing the demand.[8]

8. Richard Muth has argued that slum housing exists largely because there is a demand for it, and that efforts to reduce the supply without assisting poor families to buy better housing will reduce rather than increase their well-being. See his "Slums and Poverty," in A. A. Nevitt (ed.), *The Economic Problems of Housing* (London: Macmillan, 1967).

We conclude that the imperfections of the capital market which inhibit it from reallocating assets between users (the costs of lending and
leasing operations under conditions of uncertainty) with different opportunity costs of capital (due in turn, to unequal distribution of wealth
and progressive taxation) can cause too much land to be withheld from
its currently most profitable use. Differences in the opportunity cost of
capital, even after borrowing and lending, make renting a more attractive means of obtaining accommodation, and this in turn favors the
building of apartments. If it is judged that these differences in discount
rates are greater than are justified by the costs of lending under uncertainty, or that the uncertainty itself is unnecessarily great, it follows that
apartment development is being unduly stimulated. However, rental
housing is a logical way for "lenders" to sell capital services to "borrowers" at moderate marketing cost, with less risk of loss of capital
value than where money is lent, and to the mutual advantage of both.
Gaffney[9] has pointed out that since land is the longest lived asset, its
allocation between "borrowers" and "lenders" is most affected by capital market imperfections. But it is also less subject to erosion and more
easily administered than other assets. Hence, land can probably be
"lent" more cheaply than any other asset. It is its own very good security. We can come to only very guarded general conclusions which depend more on what we regard as an acceptable level of market perfec-
tion than on any clearly demonstrated inefficiencies.

External effects of land use decisions.   The value of a plot of urban land
is largely a function of the use of other land in the vicinity. In one sense,
then, external effects of individual decisions, which economists generally treat as rather unusual aberrations, are the essence of the urban land
market. If it were not for the fact that some nearby land was used to
provide shopping, recreational, and cultural facilities, and still other land
provided employment, the plot would not be urban at all and would
have no urban value. One way in which externalities affect development
is by putting a premium on very large-scale projects: the favorable
effects which the development or redevelopment of one lot have on the
value of the next lot can be pocketed by their common owner. By comparison, small-scale development suffers from a great deal of uncertainty
about what is going to happen to other land in the vicinity.

One of the functions which planning is supposed to perform is the
reduction of uncertainty about the future use of nearby land. In practice, this function is performed largely by zoning. An application to re-

9. Gaffney, *op. cit.*

zone a plot of land from single-family housing to apartments is frequently opposed by the residents of surrounding single-family houses, indicating that they believe that apartments will have unfavorable effects on the desirability of their houses. This belief will be considered in two parts: in this section the direct interaction will be examined, and Chapter 7 will discuss the effects of apartments on facilities provided by local governments and on the revenue and expenditure of local governments.

These single-family house owners have a legitimate complaint because their reasonable expectations have not been fulfilled. However, their expectations were presumably based on zoning, a function of local government which will be discussed in the next chapter. Direct effects of apartment developments on single-family house dwellers usually relate to aesthetics and the transient commitment of apartment dwellers to the community, which is supposed to lower the community spirit. The fact that single-family house owners neither like the people who live in apartments, nor the appearance of the apartments, may be a good reason to keep them apart as far as possible. However, there are arguments in the other direction. A mixture of low- and high-density developments can be more attractive than large areas of either. It may also be socially desirable that older, richer, and more stationary home owners should not be completely separated from the younger, poorer, and more transient members of the community. In any case, the arguments do not seem to be very important in general as long as standards of design and reasonable compatability are maintained. However, they can be important for individual house owners who find the environment unattractive. Even if their house does not lose value the social costs of moving can be high.

There can be some unfavorable short-run interactions within the private sector if a sudden increase in the number of apartments causes undue crowding of private facilities, such as shops or bowling alleys. However, these effects are not likely to last long, and are very likely to become favorable as the increase in the size of the local market makes it economic to provide a greater range of facilities.

There are two possible ways in which individual landowners can cooperate to ensure that unfavorable land use changes do not occur in their vicinity. One way is by deed covenants in which a group of landowners agree to write restrictions on its use into their property deeds. These have sometimes been struck down by the courts after many years but can be quite effective. Each landowner, as quid pro quo for foregoing a possible profitable sale, gets an assurance that others will do the same, and this may be valuable if the sale was to be for a use with undesirable external effects.[10] The second method—restrictive zoning—will be discussed in the next chapter.

The possibility of internalizing the external gains from development has several important implications. One of the important problems of redevelopment of deteriorated areas is that many of the benefits accrue to surrounding landowners rather than to the redeveloper.[11] In such areas it is difficult and expensive to accumulate a site large enough even to approach the level of self-containment which can be achieved in suburban areas. Since the land is expensive, large amounts of capital are required and the delay in establishing title, the difficulties of dealing with "hold-outs," and the problems of resettlement of the existing residents also inhibit this type of development. Not only are the positive effects of internalizing external beneficial effects more difficult to achieve in inner areas, but the negative effects of other types of land use on surrounding lots are more harmful. At the worst, the apartment areas will be surrounded by low-income single-family houses or apartments; at the best, these will be relatively new. But the new apartment in the central area is likely to be surrounded by the same type of deteriorated housing which it replaces.

Since land used for apartments is more valuable than land used for single-family housing, the gains to the larger developer of apartments in the suburbs are likely to be greater per acre, though not necessarily greater over all, than to the large-scale house builder. However, the apartment developer can hold his apartments after development to reap the continued appreciation he anticipates. In part this is in excess (that is, of what the market anticipates), and in part it represents an opportunity to convert income into capital gains. This option is not open to the house builder who, on completion, virtually has to sell to buyers with less interest in, and a lower valuation of, future capital gains.

Monopoly and imperfect competition.   Whenever a single firm or organization has control of a considerable part of the supply of a commodity that has no very close substitute, a smaller supply than is desirable is likely to be put on the market. In large, and probably even in fairly small cities, ownership of land within and around the urban area is quite widely distributed, making it impracticable for landowners to

10. The developers of the new city of Columbia, between Baltimore and Washington, intend to use deed covenants as a major means of preventing private landowners from changing the use of their land in ways which would damage the community.

11. This problem has been discussed in some detail by Otto A. Davis and Andrew B. Whinston, "The Economics of Urban Renewal," *Law and Contemporary Problems,* Vol. 26 (Winter 1961), pp. 105–17.

agree to withhold land from the market in order to reap gains from its scarcity.

Frictions in the market. A major reason for the imperfections in the capital market is the existence of a kind of friction—the cost of making the actual transactions between lenders and borrowers, landlords and tenants. The same kind of friction operates directly in the land market. To those making transactions these costs appear as lawyers' fees, real estate commissions, and the time a buyer or seller must invest if his decision is to approach an optimum. They are high relative to the value of the property involved, especially in the case of small transactions. One reason for the high legal fees is that a parcel of land is not easy to define except in involved terminology and with the aid of maps. The title can be transferred in whole or in part in many different ways, and can be subject to many different claims. Hence, the industry of title insurance assumes some risks in guaranteeing a title or, more frequently, invests a good deal in establishing the validity of the title to land in its area of operation.

If these problems are inherent in the nature of land and if lawyers' fees do represent the cost, in terms of resources, of checking the title and carrying out the transfer of ownership, the friction they create must be accepted. But there is at least some evidence that the whole system could be simplified and that, even given the system as it stands, lawyers' fees more than cover the cost of operation. This revenue is used to subsidize other parts of their operations. A fee that it is a flat percentage of market price certainly penalizes large transactions relative to small ones.

A quite different type of friction is usually represented in the fees of the real estate agent. They include the costs of acquiring knowledge about the market and about the opportunities for selling, buying, borrowing, and leasing, and the cost of getting in contact with possible buyers or sellers. The real villain of the piece is the extreme diversity of the resource called urban land. It is not possible, for example, to quote a price for urban land, even an average price, with any meaning. Few buyers would accept a "price for good suburban housing land" as the basis for buying a plot of land, unseen. The imperfections of the urban land market are similar to those of commodity markets where each farmer brings his produce to the village market and bargains about its price with the housewife. However, the diversity of urban land has a much greater value to the community than the diversity of most other commodities and these imperfections can only be eliminated at a considerable cost.

One effect of the cost of obtaining information, and of the diversity of urban land, is that it is very illiquid. If a plot of land has to be sold quickly, it will generally bring a markedly lower price than if it can be kept on the market for a considerable length of time. One reason for this is that it takes some time for the information to get to all the possible buyers. Another is that buyers enter and leave the market and the longer the plot is on the market, the more likely it is that a buyer willing to pay more than the seller's reserve price will appear.

It is worth looking at the effects which these frictions have on the urban land market and, in particular, on the apartment market in suburban areas. Legal fees at a constant percentage of the price would favor the small (single lot or house) transaction more than if they reflected costs more closely. Certainly there are economies of scale for the buyer in obtaining information and for the seller in providing information. Thus the cost of information (advertisement) is likely to be a smaller proportion of the price for selling large tracts of fairly homogenous new houses in the suburbs than for selling individual existing houses in inner suburban or city areas. Similarly, the costs of information are much smaller in leasing a large block of apartments. Transmitting information is a labor or time-intensive process which has limited scope for mechanization. Consequently, this cost is likely to increase in importance in the future.

Information about one plot of land is useful in evaluating other plots and economies can be made by the operator who specializes in the market for land within one urban area and makes it his business to know when plots of land are likely to come onto the market and what price they are likely to bring. The operations of local government are also sufficiently complex that only someone who has invested a good deal of time can evaluate the possibility of getting a plot of land rezoned and serviced by sewers, roads, and other public facilities, and can know who to contact to get these things done.

One area in which the cost of transactions is very important is the assembly of sites where the existing subdivision of ownership makes an individually owned lot too small for development or redevelopment. Here the costs of transfer and the illiquidity of land are a considerable barrier to the buyer.

These features are imperfections in the sense that the market is costly to operate but they may not be imperfections in the sense that the cost of operation, in money terms, is greater than the resources it absorbs. They tend to favor the large-scale operation; possibly favor apartments over single-family houses; certainly inhibit assembly of sites for redevelopment; and also increase the margin between the price of existing and new houses to buyers and sellers.

chapter 7

AN OPTIMAL ROLE FOR GOVERNMENT IN THE URBAN LAND MARKET

In this chapter an attempt will be made to probe the fundamental role which government should play in the local community and, in particular, in the urban land market. The purpose is to show how a government would function if its objective was to ensure that land was used in such a way as to maximize community welfare. As the role of local government in the better distribution of income and the lessening of fluctuations in the economy is, and should be, quite small—though the efforts of central governments to achieve these objectives have local effects—they will not be considered. The role actually played by local governments will be compared with the role they should play and the effects of the differences on the allocation of land will be analyzed in Chapter 8. Because I want to use a very broad brush, I will not be concerned here with the refinements of welfare economics, in one direction, or with detailing a set of institutions to carry out an ideal policy, in the other. In the first, and major, part of this chapter it is assumed that the urban land market is to remain very largely in private hands, and ways are discussed in which policy can be fitted into, and work through, such a market. In the second part, it is suggested that a much greater degree of governmental control over land use would not necessarily be less efficient.

Operations of the Government Through the Price System

One important role of governments is the provision of goods and services that could not be produced, or produced in sufficient quantities, by private firms. The most obvious of these have been classified as public goods or social goods. They have two characteristic features: (1) there is jointness of supply between individual units of the service, so that the cost of producing an extra unit is zero or small relative to the overhead cost of supplying any of the commodity at all; and (2) it is not feasible to exclude from the benefits of the service those who do not pay a price for it—i.e., many of the benefits are external to the individual producer.[1] The so-called pure public good is of less interest here

1. For a detailed discussion of the nature of public goods, see Paul A. Samuelson, "The Pure Theory of Public Expenditure," *Review of Economics and Statistics,* Vol. XXXVI (1954), pp. 387–90; and John G. Head, "Public Goods and Public Policy," *Public Finance,* Vol. XVII (1962), pp. 197–219.

than goods and services which have some of these features—semi-public goods.

Jointness of supply, often in the form of economies of scale, occurs in many sectors of the local economy. The control of air and water pollution lies at one extreme, at which the number of recipients of the benefits does not affect the cost. The local supermarket is at the other; here there are economies of scale but also competition from other supermarkets located some distance away. Between these extremes we find most of the services provided by local governments and public utilities, such as roads, water, electricity, sanitation, education, and so on. Whether these services are provided by governments or by private firms depends to a considerable extent on whether the second characteristic of pure public goods—the infeasibility of exclusion—is also present. In any case, all of these local services share a common problem, with respect to pricing, which can logically be discussed before the problem of externalities.

In industries where economies of scale are small relative to the size of the market, competitive firms set prices equal to the cost of producing a marginal extra unit. In a world where many other conditions also hold, this cost is equal to the value of the goods which could have been produced if the resources had been used in another industry. Since consumers will only pay this price if they value the goods more highly than alternatives, a price equal to long-run marginal cost will result in an optimal allocation of resources.[2] But wherever economies of scale, relative to the size of the local market, are important, a price equal to long-run marginal cost, even with peak period differentials, will not cover the total cost of production. Some part of the overhead costs will remain. As long as the difference is not too great—for example, in the case of the local supermarket—we are prepared to live with prices that are somewhat above marginal costs. But where the difference is greater (for example, water, roads), we either provide the service publicly or regulate the prices and the level of service of a privately owned utility.

One reason why prices equal to long-run marginal costs do not cover total costs is because the service may have a number of dimensions, and conventional marginal cost pricing is only concerned with one of these. In the case of water, the product is not only gallons of water but also a connection with a certain capacity to deliver water. The urban road system produces vehicle miles of travel at specific times and

2. A more detailed discussion of the "other conditions" that must hold may be found in any text on welfare economics; e.g., William J. Baumol, *Welfare Economics and the Theory of the State* (2nd ed.; Harvard University Press, 1965).

also access to a large number of properties at varying densities. It seems sensible to charge property owners with the cost of a connection to an existing main, and subdividers or eventual owners are frequently required to pay the cost of access roads, sidewalks, water, and sewerage mains for properties being developed. This kind of policy is a necessary part of marginal cost pricing and, because the presence of mains and access roads increases the value of the property, it is equitable.

Some difficulties occur when these services are provided in areas where property ownership has already become so fragmented that a collective decision is needed to install, increase the capacity, or improve the quality of the "mains" (including the access roads). Mancur Olson[3] has published an illuminating investigation of the problems that arise when decisions have to be taken collectively. If collective benefits exceed costs, it is more likely that a decision will be made to buy the "main" if the group is small and if the decision of the group is binding on all members; i.e., they have to pay whether or not they vote in favor of, and/or use the facility. When this type of pricing is in operation, and much greater use is made of special assessments, the cost of holding vacant land in an area which is being provided with urban services would be quite high. As an alternative to special assessments on all property at the time the main is installed, the full cost can be borne by those who want to use the service immediately, and other property owners will then bear a share of the capital cost, plus interest, at the time they make use of the service. All owners with a contingent liability should still share in the decision. The only difference is that it would not be necessary for the owners of undeveloped property to borrow in order to pay the special assessed charges in advance of using the service. In this case, those owners who want to make use of the service at an early stage are forced to lend to those who want to use it later.

The same arguments apply to utilities which are supplied privately. If the cost of the mains and connections for electricity, gas, and telephones were recovered from charges made against the properties served, and if marginal cost were charged for services provided, a smaller part of overhead costs would remain uncovered than if only "marginal cost per gallon" were charged. In the former case, some overhead costs of headworks type expenditures, freeways, and major distributors may remain uncovered,[4] or it may be found that the cost of collecting marginal-cost

3. Mancur Olson, *The Logic of Collective Action* (Harvard University Press, 1965).
4. It is by no means clear that charges equal to marginal cost of each dimension of services will not cover total costs of most services in large and even medium-sized cities. The case of telephone service is examined by David A. Bowers and Wallace F. Lovejoy in "Disequilibrium and Increasing Costs: A Study of Local Telephone Service," *Land Economics,* Vol. 41 (1965), pp. 31–40.

prices—e.g., for roads—exceeds the benefits in improved resource allocation. Equity and, for a private utility, efficient investment decision making, demand that remaining overheads be covered from charges on users. But short-run efficiency requires that these charges should not be proportional to use, and ideally should have no influence on the level of use. Unfortunately, these two conditions are almost mutually exclusive, because any charge on users only will dissuade some potential users from making use of the service. In the case of electricity and water, this is probably not very serious because they are almost always used. The two-part tariff can achieve both short-run efficiency and cover all overhead. Some possible solutions in other cases range from variants of the two-part tariff—such as a registration charge for cars, though this does discourage some road users—to a direct subsidy out of public funds—e.g., for public transport. Although this latter solution has often been adopted by default, it can be defended. It would be consistent with efficiency if the tax could be raised in ways which did not misallocate resources.[5] This objective is achieved by a tax on land values, which has the added attraction of not being too inequitable. All property in the general area served by a utility benefits from the availability of roads, sewers, water, electricity, and telephones.

Once charges have been set equal to marginal costs, wherever it pays to do so, including peak hour differentials,[6] it seems to be a matter of judgment how best to cover any remaining costs, if there are any. In some cases a two-part tariff may be better, and in others worse, than a public subsidy from land or other taxes. Income distribution can also be taken into account. In Chapter 8, the emphasis will be on charges which are less than marginal cost—which, from the point of view of allocation, are unambiguously bad.[7]

When some or all of the benefits of the service accrue to consumers who cannot be excluded if they do not pay, a similar problem arises. As in the case of large overheads, some part of the total cost cannot be attributed to particular buyers, but in both cases something can be done to identify the group of buyers who benefit. The extreme of either

5. The case was made in the classic article by Harold Hotelling, "The General Welfare in Relation to Problems of Taxation and of Railway and Utility Rate," *Econometrica*, Vol. 6 (1938), pp. 242–69.

6. The peak-period pricing problem has been discussed by many writers; e.g., Marcel Boiteux in "Peak-Load Pricing," *Journal of Business*, Vol. 33, No. 2 (1960), pp. 157–79, reprinted in J. R. Nelson (ed.), *Marginal Cost Pricing in Practice* (Prentice Hall, 1964).

7. It is certainly possible to imagine situations in which, because the price of a closely competitive product is too low, a price below marginal cost may improve resource allocation. William J. Baumol has commented on these problems in "Informed Judgment, Rigorous Theory and Public Policy," *Southern Economic Journal*, Vol. 32 (October 1965), pp. 137–45.

case, where no costs can be charged to particular users (pure public goods) is quite rare. There is usually some marginal cost of supplying a particular consumer with services, and some part of the services are to his individual benefit. The only acceptable reasons for setting price below this cost would be if the benefits from more rational consumption decisions were outweighed by the cost of actually recording and collecting the charge, or if considerations other than allocation are important; e.g., a desire that a service should be available to all, regardless of income.

Sometimes, as in the case of a neighborhood park, the benefits are mainly confined to those living in a small area, and consequently the value of property in that area will tend to rise, and a charge on the value of nearby land is an appropriate way of recovering the cost. In other cases, such as education, the benefits are much more widespread and subsidies from state or federal government would be needed to recover the costs from a community as wide as that which is benefited. But any "ideal" system of the type we are talking about would include a large role for user charges, special assessments on the value of land, and general taxes on land within a municipality or a metropolitan area.

External effects of particular activities are by no means always beneficial: pollution of water and air with matter and noise are conventional examples of external diseconomies. There are good reasons to tax these activities in order both to discourage them from creating harmful effects and to try to compensate for any cost of purification borne by some government. Most of the external costs associated with particular land uses affect areas nearby with particular severity. External economies are also very often felt mainly in the area close to the activity whether it be a park, a playground, or even a public library. So far I have ignored the spatial dimension in these effects. If, for instance, a park has more favorable effects in one location than in another, then the park planners should place it there. However, if the external effects of a private sports center, or a noisy factory, vary from place to place, the location decision will be affected to a limited extent by the influence exerted by owner-speculators, although problems can often arise when a speculator negotiates with a group of landowners, each of whom may be affected in a different way. One important function of urban planning is to ensure that the interests of the community as a whole, or groups within it, are taken into account in individual land use decisions.

Forecasting and control. If planners had perfect foresight they could devise an urban plan which would provide for all possible demands for sites for different land uses and arrange them in an optimal way. If they also had enough knowledge of the interactions, and enough information and computer capacity, they could program urban development so that land uses would be related to one another in the best way at each stage of development. Without perfect information and foresight this is not possible. But, in making a public or private land use decision, it is essential to forecast the use of other land in the vicinity. The discussion of land use decisions on pp. 105–8 demonstrated the very close relationship between the best use of different areas of land. The second important function of urban planning, then, is to assist in co-ordinating decisions of private and public land users. This can best be done by forecasting expected changes in land use as far into the future as possible. The main purpose of this forecasting would be to improve the decisions made by private land users and by the public sector in provision of facilities.

These two functions, forecasting and control, should be separated as far as possible, and perhaps should be administered by different parts of the planning organization. Separate branches of government quite often pursue different objectives with a single group in the community. In many countries, for example, government-employed extension officers advise farmers on how to improve their own decision making while another part of the government influences agricultural production in the presumed national interest.

The purpose of the forecasting function is to improve the efficiency of location decisions, and one of its objectives is the maximization of private profit. Forecasting should be performed in very close collaboration with, and to assist, those who are planning the location and capacity of future schools, roads, parks, and sewer and water mains. Forecasts might take the form of projected use changes in each three-year period of the coming fifteen years, with major revisions at least every three years and, perhaps, minor revisions annually. One task might be to forecast how the "control planners" might react to a proposal for a particular land use in a particular area: it would not be predicted that a noisy factory would be located in a residential area, even though the factory owner might find such a location profitable.

I would judge that the control system can best be operated through a system of variable taxes and subsidies which would not exercise absolute control but, rather, would seek to influence land use decisions. The community interest is partial more often than it is overriding. If it is agreed that the whole community has an interest in the use of private land, it seems sensible to recognize that interest by granting the local community part ownership of all land through a land value tax. This endowment of land would be the bench mark from which the variable tax or subsidy would operate. The system should be flexible because it is not possible to foresee the future and because the three alternatives currently available to influence land use—complete prohibition of a particular use, permission, or public purchase of the land—are much too restrictive. A flexible system would fill in the gaps by permitting the use, subject to paying a penal rate of tax (between permission and prohibition), or by encouraging another use through partial or complete remission of the taxes or a subsidy.

In principle, the level of taxation or subsidy would come up for review whenever the use of a plot of land was changed. In practice, the general level of taxes would only be varied when a land use would have adverse external effects or when a private landowner requested a tax remission or subsidy to use his land for some purpose which had beneficial external effects. Both the level of penal taxation and the possible level of subsidy would vary between locations and the initiative for, say, a lending library in an area might come from the local government with the offer of a subsidy, or from an entrepreneur with a request for a subsidy.

In this system, the complete prohibition in some areas of, for example, high-rise apartments would be made as widely known as possible and taken into account in forecasting but would not be formalized in anything like a zoning map. Although this might lead to changes in the value of land as the policy changed, it is impossible to maintain a rigid policy in the varying conditions of a city, and it is as well to have it known that no policy is irreversible. Setting the level of tax or subsidy would be a political decision and would sometimes be achieved by a process of bargaining. For example, the local government might be interested in getting a local gymnasium with the smallest possible subsidy, or in getting the largest possible tax revenue from a shopping center developer—in effect, putting the privilege up for auction. This type of arrangement would be an acknowledgment that private landowners and the community at large are really partners in the use of land and that together they can determine its best use. The interest of the private landowner is limited to the value of the land and can be purchased by the public, but the interest of the public is unlimited. Its part of the partnership cannot be bought out.

One problem that could arise is that the political body that determines the level of tax or subsidy might not be sufficiently responsive to the desires of small groups of affected landowners. Say a builder wanted to build apartments in a single-family area and was opposed by the other landowners. The external costs might not be large enough to warrant exclusion but might still justify a penal tax on land value.

Strictly, the tax revenue should be distributed to the affected land-owners to compensate them if there is a harmful effect on the environment. On the other hand, the revenue might be required to enable the capacity of schools, sewers, or water mains to be increased. This type of transaction occurs informally at present when, for instance, a land-owner offers part of his land for a school if he is permitted to build apartments on the remainder. This kind of agreement brings advantages to both sides. There seems to be no reason why it should not become much more common, or why it should be limited to crude bargains in which no money changes hands.

The forecasting and the control functions are very closely related in some ways. The external disadvantages which result from a particular land use decision usually depend on whether it could have been antici-pated by other landowners. If a house owner built his house with the full knowledge that an apartment would probably to built on the next lot, he deserves no compensation when the apartment is built, and it is less likely that the harmful effects will be important. The further in advance land use changes are anticipated, the more opportunity there is for different uses to be co-ordinated by the market in ways that maxi-mize the favorable and minimize the unfavorable interactions. But if this is to be taken into account in determining the level of penal tax and in deciding whether compensation will be given to existing land-owners who would be adversely affected, it is necessary to give the land use projections a good deal of formality. If an apartment is built in an area where apartment building has been the projected use for some time, the builder is less likely to have to pay a penal tax. This would offset the cost advantage of lower land values if he had bought land at its value for single-family housing and then got permission to build multiple-family housing.

Another reason for the tendency of forecasts to be self-fulfilling is that they would also be the basis for the planning of utilities and public investment. Thus, an industrialist or apartment builder could be assured of an adequate level of public facilities if he built on land with the appropriate projected use. There would be no tax penalty to compen-sate for the inadequate capacity of public facilities for the apartment builder who located in accord with the projections. The better and more effective the forecasts, the less need there would be for an active control policy.

This would not mean that the penal tax would be zero as long as land use was in accord with the forecast. Unless charges were devised to discourage pollution, noise, and unattractive appearance, certain com-mercial and industrial land users might have to pay some penal tax wherever they located. To be sure of paying no penal tax, a land use would have to be in accord with the forecast and have no adverse effects on other land users, as defined by some kind of law on nuisance, or by building regulations, etc.

On the face of it, there would seem to be scope for a local government to act as a monopoly and capture for itself as much as possible of the net returns of land users. It might be dangerous to give these powers to metropolitan-wide authorities, but with the present degree of balkanization the danger in the opposite direction is probably greater; namely, that municipalities would use the powers too lavishly in order to attract desirable land users in competition with their neighbors. Any site for a shopping center has a limited "natural monopoly" value in a community. It is possible and sensible for the local community, rather than a fortunate landowner, to capture this value by bargaining with developers. This can be achieved without restricting the number of shopping center sites below the optimum. There is scope for mismanagement and some incentive to corruption within the scheme, but on the other hand it provides a mechanism for the different interests in land use decisions to be expressed in legal bargaining rather than to be distorted into illegal or, at best, devious forms. Such powers would give a local community a great deal of freedom to plan and to develop in any desired direction and could provide a greater role for city planners. However, a community would be able, if it chose, to exercise very little control.

The local government would encourage land uses which maximized land value, since its revenue would increase with increased land value. It would tend only to give concessions in taxation, or pay out subsidies, when the land use involved would increase the value of other land in the vicinity enough to compensate for the loss of revenue. And, conversely, it would only impose penal taxes where the value of other land was threatened. From the point of view of maximizing local welfare, this seems to be quite a good criterion. It does not solve the problems of competition between local government areas, and this might have undesirable effects on the welfare of particular groups. In particular, there might be an increase in the barriers which presently prevent poor families and minority groups from moving out of their ghettos. There might also be very strong competition between parts of a city for the office employment and clean light industry which bring prosperity.[8] The richer municipalities would be able to outbid the poorer. A solution to these problems must be sought at a higher level of government through

8. Bernard J. Frieden, "Towards Equality of Urban Opportunity," *Journal of the American Planning Institute,* Vol. 31 (1965), pp. 320–30.

grants which benefit poorer local governments,[9] or transference of functions to a higher level of government, laws which prevent discrimination, and co-ordination of development between the jurisdictions within a metropolitan area when the development has metropolitan significance. Any policy which does not change the underlying distribution of income, responsibilities, and "rights" is unlikely to solve this problem finally.

The suggested system might be made clearer by considering a particular case, almost as it might pass through the administrative system. Take an application to build apartments in an area of single-family housing. If apartments have been projected for the area for some considerable time, say at least ten years, and if the proposed apartment does not have any unusual features—such as high density or a very high building—which would have adverse effects locally, it is approved without further investigation. The approval is made public and the organizations providing utilities, schools, roads, etc., are notified so that they can be ready to provide the necessary capacity if it is not already available. Like a building permit, the approval would have a limited life and would only be valid for the type of building approved.

If apartments have only recently been projected for the area, other landowners in the area have the right to make representation for compensation, and this will vary depending on the loss of amenity they will suffer and the period that has elapsed since the projected use was changed. If the projected use of the area was for single-family housing, owners have the same right, and organizations providing public services can also demand compensation for the unexpected cost of providing for increased capacity. Taking these factors into account, the land use control board will set some level of penal tax, part of which might be offset by reducing taxation for house owners who will be adversely affected, and part used to enlarge the capacity of public services. If the penal tax is too high for the prospective developer, he will withdraw his application or, if the board considers that the harmful effects are greater than the value of the land, it could refuse permission outright. If large capital sums are required to increase the capacity of public services, it would be reasonable to require that part of the penal tax be capitalized as a lump sum charge.

Certain types of recreational facilities might be provided by a private developer with the aid of a subsidy. A developer might propose to build tennis courts, make them available free of charge during the day,

9. The United Kingdom's block grants to local governments seek to achieve this. See R. G. D. Allen (Chairman), *Committee of Inquiry into the Impact of Rates on Households,* Cmnd. 2582 (London: Her Majesty's Stationery Office, 1965).

and charge for their use in the evenings and at weekends. The local government might consider that this plan warrants a subsidy because of the free recreation provided for children during the day and might wish to control the level of charges during peak demand periods.

I introduced this analysis by using the theory of public goods as a point of departure. The part of that theory which deals with externalities can also be linked to that part of applied welfare economics which deals specifically with this problem. It has long been recognized that, in an unregulated private market, an activity which produces harmful external effects would be carried on at too high a level, while one which produces beneficial external effects would not produce enough.[10] The conventional prescription for dealing with this problem was to tax producers of harmful external effects and subsidize producers of beneficial external effects in order to equalize marginal private cost and marginal social cost. The disadvantage of this prescription is that it ignores the income effects, both on those who are harmed by the harmful effects or by the tax needed to finance the subsidy, and on those who benefit from the beneficial effects or from the remission of other taxes. They are unlikely to be the same people.

A better way of approaching ideal resource allocation is to permit those who produce the external effects to bargain with those who are affected, both about the level of compensation which must be paid from one to the other, and about the level of production. In some cases the result may be the payment of compensation without any change in the level of production; in others, production might stop altogether where there are harmful external effects, and might be started where there are no harmful effects or where there are external beneficial effects.[11] One major disadvantage of the bargaining solution is that it depends on the relative bargaining strengths of the parties involved and on the number of persons affected. We cannot assume that a large number of landowners, all of whom are affected a little, will bargain in the same way as a single landowner on whom the same total effects are concentrated.[12] The typical situation in the urban land market is when a change in the use of the property of one owner will affect a relatively large number of others.

The system I have suggested uses taxes and subsidies as a means of

10. Classically described by A. C. Pigou, *The Economics of Welfare* (4th ed.; London: Macmillan, 1932).

11. R. H. Coase, "The Problem of Social Costs," *Journal of Law and Economics,* Vol. 3 (October 1960), pp. 1–44; Otto A. Davis and Andrew B. Whinston, "Some Notes on Equating Private and Social Costs," *Southern Economic Journal,* Vol. 32 (1965), pp. 113–26.

12. See Olson, *op. cit.*

bargaining but gives the task of bargaining to a local government body, charged with representing the interests of all landowners who might be affected by any land use change. In this way, the relative strengths of the bargaining parties become more equal and a formal organization is responsible for representing the total interests of the group. The role of law is to specify the initial position from which bargaining starts; i.e., the rights of each partner. This was previously mentioned in discussions on the conditions under which a landowner would have the right to use his land for a particular purpose without any penal tax, and the conditions under which affected landowners would have the right to demand compensation. The major determinant is the law of nuisance. Levels of compensation are adjusted according to whether the change of use was anticipated or not.

Decisions about the level of tax or subsidy might be as difficult as the decisions about rezoning that are taken at present. But, with some effort, many of the external effects could be quantified. It should not be difficult to estimate the increased cost of providing unanticipated expansion of public service capacity. With a little more effort, the effects of particular kinds of land use on the value of nearby property could be estimated.[13] Admittedly, some external effects are very difficult to quantify, but if bargaining is open there is no need to decide in black or white terms that a particular use on a particular plot is or is not in the public interest. Public and private interests usually coincide over a very large area and often conflict over a much smaller area.

One final disclaimer. This scheme is not advanced as a fully developed means of solving the problem of control of land use in metropolitan areas. For the purposes of this study it serves to define how the government could act if its objective were to promote the best allocation of land possible. We need some standard by which to judge the present performance of zoning, the pricing policies of utilities and public services, and the level of service provision. However, I do believe that a probing of the fundamental function performed by government in this area is required before the system can be made to work more efficiently in the interest of the whole community. I hope that this analysis asks some relevant questions and points toward some of the right directions for improving the system.

A Planning Solution to the Land Use Problem

Urban land is one area about which it can logically be argued that the private market works so inefficiently that the gains from complete

13. For an approach to measuring the effects of parks, see Jack L. Knetsch, "Land Values and Parks in the Urban Fringe Areas," *Journal of Farm Economics*, Vol. 44 (1962), pp. 1718–26.

public control would more than offset the losses. If all land use decisions were taken centrally, the problem of co-ordination would disappear to a large extent. Although the central authority could not expect to foresee the future perfectly, it would have much better knowledge about the future use of a great deal of land. Compensation would still be needed when unforeseen changes in land use occurred. At one level, public control of land use would eliminate the need for the complex methods outlined above of expressing the public interest in primarily private land use decisions. At another level, it can be compared with the advantages of a single private firm planning a large subdivision or a whole new town. This generally results in much better-planned communities, because the firm co-ordinates land use decisions and plans them in such a way that harmful external effects are minimized and beneficial interactions are maximized: the externalities are internalized.

Public control of land use does not necessarily mean that the government completely takes over the role of the private sector in this area. The method used in Canberra, the federal capital of Australia, is not perfect but shows that planning solutions to the land use allocation problem are practicable. All land is owned by the government. At the time of subdivision the use of each plot of land is specified and can only be changed with the permission of the planning authority. Land rents are set for each plot at 5 per cent of a conservative estimate of the market value. Ninety-nine-year leases, for which rent is established for the first twenty years and use specified, are then put up for public auction. After twenty years, rents are reassessed on the basis of changes in market values of land.

Although the land is owned publicly, private leasees buy very considerable interests in it, and these are negotiable. The market not only allocates land between individual leasees on the basis of the premium each is willing to pay, but also indirectly determines the volume of land which will be released for particular uses as the planning authority attempts to project demand. Because it has been growing so rapidly, Canberra has not yet had to face the problem of compensating owners of leases when their expectations about the future use of surrounding land are not fulfilled because the land use plan has had to be amended in the light of unforeseen changes. This problem will have to be faced. Although, because the interest of leasees in land is smaller than the interest of owners, the problem is much less acute than in cities with freehold tenure, it does not seem to be different in nature. In a planned community, the question of compensation only arises when the plan has to be changed and the problem is, therefore, less common than when land use decisions are privately made.

Some candidates for election to the Montgomery County Council suggested a betterment tax, to be levied on the increase in value of land when, by rezoning, a change in use was permitted. Even if this tax were at a rate no higher than the capital gains tax, it would be different in that it would be paid when the increase in value occurred, rather than when the land was sold. This difference can be important for a land-owner or developer since he would normally have to borrow to pay the tax. A tax at a higher rate, as proposed in the British Land Commission Bill,[14] would discourage the holding of land as compared with other appreciating assets, but would only discourage it unduly, compared with income-producing assets, if the rate of tax exceeded the land-owner's marginal income tax rate.

It has also been suggested that zoning within some general area for high-density uses, such as apartments and shopping centers, should be auctioned. This is a variant of the bargaining I have suggested. The price would be a function of the number of sites released. If planners are to decide how many, they will be performing an additional function in the land market, moving it somewhat closer to complete government control. This proposal does not go as far in government control as the alternative previously outlined. Consequently, the co-ordination function of zoning is partly lost.

The objective of both these proposals is to recover for the public purse some of the profits from rezoning. They accept a relatively large role for zoning in the control of land use. Both are more discriminatory than a land value tax, and, unlike it, would not recover a consistent proportion of all increases in land value, for whatever reason. Either proposal would probably improve on zoning as now performed (and discussed in more detail in the next chapter). My own preference is either for a system which places primary reliance on the private land market, with government only performing functions that the private land market can-not perform effectively; or for one which primarily relies on public land use decisions and allocates land, with the use already specified, to private users. But the degree of control can be varied continuously.

A community's preference for one system or another should be based, at least partly, on the grounds of efficiency. In fact, however, the choice is more likely to result from the community's values. There is no a priori reason to expect that when land use decisions are taken out of private hands, the loss of competitive drive will reduce efficiency any more than the greater co-ordination of central decision making will in-crease it.

14. Great Britain, Ministry of Land and Natural Resources, *The Land Commission,* Cmnd. 2771 (London: Her Majesty's Stationery Office, 1965).

Some inefficiencies of private decision making in the field of land use have been indicated in this chapter. Of these, some could be corrected by changes which would keep decision making decentralized, but others could not. On the other hand, the decisions of governments can also be inefficient, especially where local governments serve small areas, and therefore have few resources to devote to good decision making.

chapter 8

THE EFFECTS
OF NON-OPTIMAL
PUBLIC POLICY

In this chapter, the critical examination of the volume and location of apartment building is continued. In Chapters 2 to 4, the ways in which public policies of various kinds have influenced apartment building have been considered and questions have been asked about their effects, as part of a general attempt to find causal explanations. With Chapter 7 as a basis for comparison, the normative questions can now be asked: Has public policy encouraged too much or too little apartment building, and has it caused apartments to be built in the wrong places? For the most part, the criterion used is the best allocation of resources—in particular, land—but in one section the effect on resource allocation of inter-personal and interarea distribution of income and rights will be examined. Practically the whole of this chapter is qualitative, and policies are examined one by one. It is not possible, however, to add up the individual effects and come to a firm conclusion about the over-all effect of differences between the actual and the optimal public policies described in the previous chapter.

Charges for Utility Investment

For present purposes, utilities will be defined to include all services produced by public, or publicly controlled, bodies, the benefits from which accrue very largely to users. The major defect in present policies is that users, as such, are required to pay too little of the capital cost of utilities. Instead of charging the costs of mains and arterial streets to actual beneficiaries, either through capital charges or special taxes on the properties actually served, the charges are too frequently averaged over very large numbers of properties. Or they may be financed out of the general revenue, from direct user charges (e.g., telephones, gas) or property taxes (e.g., roads). Although I have not examined these policies in detail, it is certainly possible to see the general direction and magnitude of the effects. In the area served by the Washington Suburban Sanitary Commission, the cost of water mains is averaged over all properties served, in the form of a front foot charge.[1] But those properties

1. My source of information on the Sanitary Commission's policies is Francis X. Tannian, "Water and Sewer Supply Decisions: A Case Study of the Washington Suburban Sanitary Commission" (Unpublished Ph.D. Thesis, University of Virginia, 1965).

which are classified as farm land do not pay the front foot charge until they are subdivided, even though water mains are made available.

One result is that, given the front footage, there is no difference in water costs to users in scattered and in consolidated developments. The higher cost of mains for scattered developments is spread over all properties in the Sanitary Commission's service area in proportion to the front footage. Perhaps the demand for water is sufficiently inelastic that the charging system has little effect on demand.[2] But low-density, scattered developments could sometimes be better served from wells. Again, the charging system might not matter very much if the Sanitary Commission used a benefit-cost type of criterion in deciding when and where to extend its services, but it does not. If users were charged full costs of extensions to water supply mains, the opposition to uneconomic extensions would be expected to come largely from customers who felt that the service was not worth its cost. But, since so much of the cost is borne by others, the opposition to scattered development is much weaker than it should be.

Although water supply reticulation is sufficiently cheap and necessary that the demand is inelastic, the same cannot be said for sewerage. The capital costs of sewer mains are a major cost of subdivision. If the most economic shape, location, and timing of subdivision is to be encouraged, it is important that differences in the cost of sewers should be felt, and taken into account, by those making decisions about property development. The extent of averaging is less than in the case of water supply: the capital costs of providing sewers are averaged over the properties sewered in a particular year. Although this is an improvement on the water charging system, it is far from ideal because, in any year, some properties will involve much more expensive sewerage investment than others. Properties close to existing trunk sewers can be connected more cheaply than those further away. But this will not be reflected in charges to users. Again, scattered developments are not discouraged as much as they should be.

Recently the Washington Suburban Sanitary Commission has made some steps toward differentiating between different properties. It has required "contributions" from individual large apartment, commercial, or industrial developments which are remote from existing sewers and where, therefore, sewers would be very expensive to install. It is not clear, though, that these contributions bear a close relationship to costs.

2. Recent work by Charles W. Howe and F. Pierce Linaweaver, Jr. at Resources for the Future suggests that demand, especially for sprinkling, may be quite elastic. See Howe and Linaweaver, "The Impact of Price on Residential Water Demand and Its Relation to System Design and Price Structure," *Water Resources Research*, Vol. 3, No. 1 (1967), pp. 13–32.

They certainly could closely approach a marginal capital cost charge. More recently still, two extensive schemes have been proposed in which sewers for scattered developments would be financed from contributions from the owner of each house and apartment unit.[3] Where this was proposed in Montgomery County it was eventually dropped, perhaps because users, faced with paying the total cost of the extensions, opposed it strongly. The cost of sewering an area is not only affected by density and contiguity of development. Location is also important. The installation of expensive pumping equipment may be required and the further the property is from treatment works, the greater the costs of mains to carry the sewage. In the past, at least, there has been no serious effort to distinguish between properties on these kinds of grounds in the Sanitary Commission's service area.

It seems to be very clear that the yearly averaging and front-foot kind of charging systems encourage urban sprawl. Perhaps they encourage scattering of developments more than low-density development. Since the owners of farm land have to pay nothing for water, and the owners of vacant land do not have to pay for sewerage, the cost of holding land vacant is less than it would be with an ideal charging system. In Chapter 7, I suggested that owners of vacant land should be charged their share of the capital cost plus interest when they eventually make connection. With such a contingent liability they should have a voice in whether, and when, the extension is provided. It seems fairly clear that in Montgomery County both sewerage and water supply have been provided both over too wide an area and too soon, and that this has permitted scattered developments which otherwise would not have been economic or would have been prohibited for health reasons. This has been particularly true because the Sanitary Commission serves both Montgomery and Prince Georges counties. Montgomery County is mostly at a higher elevation—which frequently means that water has to be pumped—and is farther from sewerage treatment plants. The part of the county which is in the watershed of the Patuxent, the source of part of the counties' water, must have its sewage pumped out for treatment on the Potomac.

When charges are averaged over the two counties, Prince Georges landowners have to pay more, and Montgomery County landowners less, than cost. The Sanitary Commission claims that it only follows development, and hence does not influence it. However, many develop-

3. *Washington Post*, October 12, 1966. It is interesting that the charge is to be higher for new than for existing houses. The principle does not appear to be "cost plus interest" for later connections. Rather it is an equity consideration. Present house owners have septic tanks and it is only increasing density of development that has made them unacceptable.

ment decisions in unsewered areas are dependent on the construction
of sewers. They are important and necessary for all but low-density development. The terms on which they are provided can easily influence
location decisions. Scattered apartment developments are especially dependent on sewers, since they are too large to use septic tanks.

The major roads of Montgomery County are financed out of general
revenue, part of which is returned by the state from the fuel tax. Within
housing and apartment subdivisions, access roads are provided by developers. Once outside these subdivisions, the traffic generated by them
is fed on to roads paid for by the general public in one way or another.
If the apartment development is remote from work and shopping places,
increased capacity will be required along a greater mileage of roads. The
increase in public cost may easily exceed the private cost of increased
fuel taxes. In the long run, of course, scattered developments lead to
scattered employment and shopping, but trips are probably still longer
and there are more cross trips. Sometimes building and improving public roads which give access to property and increase its value costs far
more than the contribution made by the owner through higher property
taxes. Holding such land vacant costs the owner less than it costs the
community, and so speculative holding of vacant land and scattering
are encouraged.[4]

The practice of other utilities—such as gas, electricity, and telephones—of recovering the capital costs of their networks from users
through charges on volume of use that exceed marginal costs (gas and
electricity), or fixed rental charges (telephone), also encourages scattered
and low-density development. In these areas the network cost per connection or per unit of sales is high.[5] Although costs are higher in outlying and scattered developments, this is rarely reflected in higher
charges, and there is no contingent liability for the owners of vacant
property to pay part of the capital cost of mains plus interest.

User Charges

Under this heading levels of variable charges per unit used—e.g., per
gallon of water, or per kilowatt hour of electricity—will be discussed.

4. Note that this discussion refers specifically to "access" roads. These may be
defined as roads used at less than capacity. Robert H. Strotz's conclusions that no
land-related charges are required if user charges are optimal do not refer to this
type of road. See Strotz, "Urban Transportation Parables," in Julius Margolis (ed.),
The Public Economy of Urban Communities (Resources for the Future, Inc., 1965),
pp. 151–62.
5. Scattering of development may have a greater influence than density. The
effect of density variations could be so low as to make it not worthwhile to
differentiate charges. *The Effects of Large Lot Size on Residential Development*,
Technical Bulletin No. 32 (Urban Land Institute, 1958), has evidence about the
effect of density.

Apart from roads and public transport, most utilities are very broadly self-supporting, so that higher charges for installation of mains would permit lower user charges. In Montgomery County this is not necessarily true of water and sewerage. It is not clear that the installation charges are too low, but only that they are not correctly allocated among land-owners. The operating costs of water and sewerage were financed from charges, in 1966, of 25 and 22 cents per 1,000 gallons of water used, respectively, plus a small charge for reading the meter. Although marginal cost pricing might result in some change in the part of total costs which are covered from these charges, they seem to be an appropriate method of charging. Perhaps main sewer maintenance costs, varying with distance to the treatment plant, should vary with location rather than, or as well as, with water usage. And it may be worth metering the sewer input to avoid a sewer charge for water used for sprinkling.

User charges on roads are not optimal and this may have more important implications for the volume and location of apartment development. Apartments in suburban areas are more oriented to the automobile than are downtown apartments, and this is truer on the suburban fringe than near suburban centers. Users of roads in suburban and high land value areas pay less than the opportunity cost of the road space they use, both for travelling and for parking,[6] and this encourages them to travel at peak hours, to use automobiles rather than other means of travelling to work, and provides them with no incentive to choose work-place-home locations that involve less travel on high-cost roads. Living in a suburban house or apartment and working in the city center involves the use of very high-cost road space. Although devices have been developed to charge drivers on congested streets something closer to their opportunity costs, there is still some doubt whether the gains would be worth the cost of collection. In any case, if driving had been more expensive than public transport, especially in peak hours and in congested areas, apartment development would probably have been even greater, since apartments can more easily be concentrated close to public transport routes. However, they would have been more concentrated downtown and in suburban centers.

It is difficult to judge how large these effects would have been had "congestion charges" been in force throughout. In any case, their introduction at the present stage of urban development would have a quite different effect. By making downtown areas more difficult and costly to get to, they might accelerate the suburbanization of employment, shop-

6. I have discussed this problem in "Pricing Road Use," *Economic Record*, Vol. 40 (1964), pp. 175–86; and in "Investment Criteria and Road Pricing," *The Manchester School*, Vol. 34 (1966), pp. 63–74.

ping, etc. Rather than forsake their cars, commuters might increasingly favor jobs and shops close to their suburban homes and apartments. Congestion is not limited to downtown areas, or even to suburban centers. There is good economic justification for claiming that any road of more than two lanes that is not congested to some degree should be. Otherwise it is too wide. But the optimal level of congestion is lower where land values are low, and in most suburban areas the optimal user charge is probably no higher than the present fuel tax.

In Chapter 7 it was suggested that only collection difficulties or distributional considerations can justify prices which are less than marginal cost. By this criterion there are too few user charges for many urban services, or at least there would be if distribution could be taken care of elsewhere. The case for broadening user prices and the means by which they might be charged have been examined by others.[7] Some of the appropriate means of levying user charges have implications for spatial patterns; e.g., Vickrey suggested a fire protection user charge related to site area.

There is a good deal of evidence that apartments pay more in property taxes than the cost of the services provided.[8] But this depends to a considerable extent on the fact that families living in apartments have fewer schoolchildren than families living in single-family houses. Given that education is provided by local government, and that it is not financed by user charges, it is neither inefficient nor inequitable for families at all stages of the life cycle to contribute to the cost of education; not only the cost of their children's education while they have children at school, but also after their children have left school, and especially the cost of their own education after they themselves have left school. Families tend to occupy apartments at those stages of their life cycle when they are less likely to have children at school.

If much of the present property tax were replaced by user charges, apartments would probably be cheaper relative to single-family houses— especially the less scattered apartments where economies of scale can reduce cost of, for example, fire protection without requiring long distances between fire stations. Although apartment developers frequently

7. For example, William S. Vickrey, "General and Specific Financing of Urban Services," in Howard G. Schaller (ed.), *Public Expenditure Decisions in the Urban Community* (Resources for the Future, Inc., 1963); O. H. Brownlee, "User Prices vs. Taxes," in Universities–National Bureau Committee for Economic Research, *Public Finances: Needs, Sources, and Utilization—A Conference* (Princeton University Press, 1961); Dick Netzer, *The Economics of the Property Tax* (Brookings Institution, 1965), pp. 214–17.

8. George Sternlieb, *The Garden Apartment Development: A Municipal Cost-Revenue Analysis* (Rutgers University, Bureau of Economic Research, 1964); Office of Planning, Arlington County, Virginia, *Fiscal Aspects of Land Use, Arlington County, Virginia* (Arlington, 1957).

provide parking areas and recreation facilities and sometimes their own garbage disposal systems, apartments also frequently increase the cost of the public provision of these services. High-density apartments provide few of these facilities, but they are often occupied by families who make little use of outdoor recreation facilities of any kind. Families living in high-density apartments, especially in central cities, and even in suburban centers, are less likely to own cars and thereby to contribute to costly congestion. Outside the building, the capital cost of utility services for apartments is quite low. When these costs are averaged in some way, or loaded onto the variable user charges, apartment dwellers tend to suffer. If user charges were not rational, apartment dwellers would probably gain over all, but this would be much more true of those living in areas of high-density development than of those scattered around the urban fringe.

Property Taxes[9]

I have suggested that part of the present taxes on the improved value of property should be replaced by user charges, part by grants from state and federal governments, and the remainder by a tax on land values. I have discussed the effects of a change from a tax on total property value to a tax on land value in some detail elsewhere.[10] The only major exception to the proposition that land value taxes are neutral with respect to land use decisions occurs when developers, usually of large projects, obtain part of their return from the increase in land value during the process of development. This appears to be quite an important consideration in many apartment development projects. Under these circumstances, a land value tax will actually reduce the profitability of apartment development or increase the price of apartments if development is competitive. A simple example should illustrate this. In the absence of any tax on land value, the land appreciates from $10,000 to $30,000 when apartment zoning is gained, water and sewerage services are arranged, and, say, a shopping center development next door is negotiated. Let us assume that the "cost" of making all of these arrangements, plus interest on the capital invested during the process, absorbs the whole profit of $20,000. Next, let us introduce a land value tax equal to the rate of return on capital. This will halve the market

9. The discussion in this section is based on the assumption that the interest rate is largely independent of the property tax rate. This will be true if only some kinds of property are taxed (e.g., land or real property), or if there are considerable differences between rates of tax on different kinds of property or in different localities.

10. Max Neutze, "Property Taxation and Multiple Family Housing," to be published as part of the proceedings of a Conference on Property Taxes and Economic Development, by the University of Wisconsin Press.

value both before and after the arrangements have been made. If the developer has to pay the same cost of $20,000 to make the arrangements, he will not find it profitable to build unless he can get apartment rents so much higher that the pre-tax value of the land would be $50,000 instead of $30,000. Value with the tax would then rise from $5,000 to $25,000.

This parallels the well-known phenomenon in which a tax on land value discourages large-scale projects if the land is valued piece by piece rather than as a whole.[11] In both cases, one assumption on which the neutrality of the land value tax is based is violated; namely, that the value of land is unaffected by any actions of the landowner. In the first case, the landowner can use the expected profits to increase his land's value by inducing favorable changes elsewhere. In the second, the same landowner can own an area large enough that the value of each part is affected by the use of other parts. If apartment projects are on a large scale, or if the expected speculative profits from them are used to influence complementary uses of land nearby (and to the extent that the cost of such influences is not itself proportional to land value), a land value tax will reduce the volume of the more speculative land uses— such as apartments—relative to the less speculative—single-family housing.[12]

A land value tax endows the community with part of the value of its land. But, unlike the private landowner, the community is willing to rent its part of the value to anyone at a fixed rate of return on value and without any security requirements. Consequently, a land value tax would permit bidders with a higher opportunity cost of capital, and less wealth (security), to put in a higher relative bid for the land.[13] As a result, land and house ownership would become more widespread than renting. Since ownership is still mainly confined to houses and renting to apartments, this would reduce apartment building, particularly in suburban areas where house builders would more often be successful in bidding for land. In central areas many older houses are rented but if more were owned, thus avoiding the administrative costs of renting, there would be more incentive to renovate. Redevelopment would also be stimulated by lower land prices. It is not at all obvious whether the

11. Edwin R. A. Seligman, *The Shifting and Incidence of Taxation* (Columbia University Press, 1926), Chapter 3.
12. The term speculative here has the same special meaning as in earlier chapters. A speculative land user expects more of his return to come through increased land values, relative to income earning possibilities that are not expected to vary over time.
13. M. Mason Gaffney, "The Unwieldy Time-Dimension of Space," *The American Journal of Economics and Sociology,* Vol. 20 (1961), pp. 465–81.

over-all effect would be the increase or the reduction of central area apartment building.

The most effective part of a change in the means of financing public services may be the lifting of the tax on improvements to land. Although many studies have failed to find any empirical effect of differences in real estate tax rates, there are quite strong reasons for believing that tax levels do have some effect, particularly where the rates are high.[14] Improvements are discouraged when taxed, and particularly when the rate of taxation is high. This is frequently so in the central cities because the level of expenses is highest there. Since housing absorbs a significant proportion of family budgets, especially those of the poorer families which often predominate in central cities, it seems almost certain that there is some elasticity in the demand for housing. If improvements were relieved of property tax, the result might not be spectacular progress in urban renewal and renovation, but there would probably be some. Housing standards might be greatly improved as overcrowding was reduced.

Single-family houses are a land-intensive form of accommodation, while apartments are a building-intensive form. Even when land zoned for apartments is more valuable than that zoned for houses (because of the quasi-monopoly advantage which zoning gives), the cost of apartment land per dwelling unit ($2,000 to $3,000 in Washington suburbs) is still less than the cost (say $5,000) of a lot for a single-family house in anything like a comparable location. The structure constitutes a higher proportion of the cost of apartments than it does of single-family houses, and consequently the removal of the tax from capital structures built on land would reduce the costs of apartments relative to single-family houses. In central areas, apartments are built at greater densities because of higher land values, and the capital cost per unit is higher than for suburban apartments. Removal of the tax would mean a greater reduction of costs in central areas, and it is at least possible that families which live in these areas might use their resultant higher real income to switch toward lower-density living in suburban housing, despite the relative rise in its cost. But apartment living probably is not such an "inferior good" as that.

14. Morris Beck failed to find a relationship between level of tax and land use changes in "Urban Redevelopment: Influence of Property Taxation and Other Factors," *Proceedings of the Fifty-Seventh Annual Conference on Taxation . . . 1964* (Harrisburg, Pa., 1965), pp. 239–49. But M. Mason Gaffney, "Property Taxes and the Frequency of Urban Renewal," *ibid.*, pp. 272–85, and Dick Netzer, *The Economics of the Property Tax, op. cit.*, pp. 67–85, give persuasive reasons for believing that it has effects on land use decisions. Netzer presents evidence that apartments, especially large buildings, are presently taxed at a higher effective rate than single-family houses.

As compared with almost any uniform system of property taxation, farm land assessment, as practiced in Maryland, encourages the withholding of land on the urban fringe from development. By engaging in farming, perhaps only in a token way, owners of land on the urban fringe can have their land assessed as if its most profitable use for the foreseeable future was for farming.[15] A tax on land is, in part, a capital gains tax at a rate equal to the tax rate, divided by itself plus the rate at which the market discounts future returns from the land. But when the amount of tax is invariant with changes in the market value of land, the capital gains tax disappears. There is a tax on the conversion of the land to urban uses, but this can be postponed until the change actually occurs. There is no obligation to repay the tax concession. In terms of the short-run land use model shown in Chapter 6, the profitability of postponing conversion will be increased by a tax on the value of land used for urban purposes which is not paralleled by a tax on the value it gains from expected future urban use. The cost to the community of holding vacant land in urban areas may not be fully reflected in the present property taxes. But when they, too, are greatly reduced by special assessment, speculation in vacant land is profitable more often than it is socially desirable.

If land is held vacant while it is approached, and sometimes surrounded, by urbanization, sites ideally suited to apartments or shopping centers are sometimes produced. It may be difficult to maintain even token farming until apartments are built, but if the costs of holding land are reduced for only part of the time by making use of farm land assessment, the resultant larger capital gains can be divided between the original landowner and the developer, and competition can turn these into cheaper apartments. Because apartments are a more speculative use of land, they are more favored than single-family housing by farm land assessment, especially if "farming" can be maintained while apartment zoning is gained.

Owners who would farm the land may be less able to wait for returns while they bear high taxes than other potential owners. Hence, farm land assessment probably increases the amount of agriculture practiced on the urban fringe—given the problems of speculators renting to farmers. The encouragement to undue withholding would be much smaller and agriculture would be encouraged as much if the tax liability was postponed rather than remitted.

15. Peter House, *Preferential Assessment of Farmland in the Rural-Urban Fringe of Maryland,* ERS-8 (U.S. Department of Agriculture, Economic Research Service, 1961).

Externalities

One of the important justifications for planning is that some land uses have unfavorable and others favorable external effects on the users of other land in the vicinity. When decision makers are considering a particular use for a plot of land, they have to decide—either well before the event, when zoning maps are drawn, or when rezoning applications are considered—whether the location chosen is one in which the external benefits are maximized, and/or the external costs minimized. This is very difficult to predict far in advance. It is even more difficult to defend when an applicant applies for rezoning. Traditional zoning, as a means of controlling land use, makes it necessary to say either yes or no to an application. Although it is often used, sometimes informally, the legality of conditional zoning is rather doubtful. An activity may have undesirable external effects in any location, but it can be located anywhere in the appropriate zone (which should, of course, contain activities that will be least unfavorably affected) without paying any compensation to those it injures. An application for rezoning can be denied if it is believed that the external injurious effects are too great, but if it is granted, there is no compensation for unforeseen injurious effects to those who are affected. An applicant can change his application for rezoning to minimize injurious effects, but there is no formal means by which affected property owners can recoup their losses. Sometimes informal and rather clumsy bargaining occurs. For example, in a case in Montgomery County, an apartment developer offered to give some land to adjacent single-family house owners as a "shield" against the injurious effects of his apartments. (The shield would also benefit apartment dwellers.) Although the offer was made to appear as if external effects were being reduced, the gift of land could equally well be regarded as compensation for damages. However, house owners a little further away, who were concerned about increased congestion of streets and other neighborhood facilities, could not be bought off by any such convenient compensation. Since there was no way in which compensation could be made to look like "good planning," they continued to oppose the rezoning and remained uncompensated and unhappy.

Where a land use has a favorable external effect, there is an equal lack of any direct means by which it can be encouraged. Consequently, facilities which might have been provided privately with a modest subsidy have to be provided wholly out of public funds. On the other hand, they may be provided publicly, but largely financed from charges for use. It makes no difference in principle whether management is public or private. The federal government has moved further in this direction than local governments; it has, for example, granted subsidies for open space.

Some apartment developers might be encouraged, by a modest subsidy, to provide better recreation facilities and to open them to the public. One proposed move in this direction in Montgomery County is to give tax concessions to property owners who would grant scenic easements to the county. This would seem to make sense as a subsidy to encourage a land use of value to the public. It is being opposed on the grounds that it can be used as a means of evading taxes while land is held for speculative purposes. This suspicion is partly due to the fact that the farm land assessment concession, which was promoted for similar reasons, has been used to greatly benefit land speculators. It has been confirmed by the provision that the existence of the easement shall not reduce the condemnation value of a property purchase by a government. Easements of this type, or any plan, should not be irrevocable, because it is not possible to foresee the future completely. The principle is useful but requires safeguards to prevent its abuse.

What can be said about the external effects of apartments on other land users? Most retailers and employers probably welcome the building of apartments nearby because of the high concentration of potential customers, on the one hand, and the increased pool of potential employees, on the other. There appear to have been two sides to arguments about the effects of apartments on the level of taxes which other landowners would have to pay. Studies in both Arlington and Montgomery counties are consistent with the results of studies in other parts of the country.[16] In general, apartments are more fiscally profitable than single-family houses. They may pay more or less to the local public account than their residents receive, depending on the volume of commercial and industrial property, which almost always shows a fiscal profit. Where there is a good deal of commerce and industry, apartments may be "unprofitable," but single-family houses are more so.

Fiscal profit is not necessarily a good reason for encouraging apartment growth. First, since it depends very largely on the family structure of apartment dwellers, there is no logical reason to encourage families to live in apartments rather than in houses. They will probably produce a greater fiscal profit if they live in houses, and the type of housing probably has little causal effect on numbers of children. Even from such a narrow viewpoint, apartments should be encouraged only when families with no, or few, children can be attracted from other jurisdictions. Second, as pointed out in some detail by Julius Margolis,[17] fiscal profit-

16. See footnote 6 on p. 142. The Montgomery County study was limited to school-children but it implies similar conclusions. The Maryland National Capital Park and Planning Commission, *Apartments and their Impact on the Public Elementary Schools in the Maryland-Washington Regional District of Montgomery and Prince Georges County,* Technical Bulletin No. 10 (June 1959).

17. Julius Margolis, "On Municipal Policy for Fiscal Gains," *National Tax Journal,* Vol. 9 (1956), pp. 247–57.

ability is not a good criterion for choosing the way a community should grow. The government is not the only sector of the economy, nor is it so important that its advantages and disadvantages should be given overriding weight. Particular land uses may contribute to local community welfare in ways which are quite independent of the tax revenue they produce, and may bring disadvantages quite apart from the public spending they necessitate. The fact that some land uses are fiscally profitable and others a fiscal liability shows one or both of two things: (1) The taxing and charging system for local public goods is non-optimal—we have seen that this is frequently true. (2) Functions such as education, health, and welfare, which are not financed from user charges because of external economies and because they are used to redistribute income, have spillover effects across jurisdictional boundaries. There is an incentive for jurisdictions to attract families for which these costs will be low, and to attract land uses (and families) which are the recipients of favorable inter-jurisdictional spillovers. This possibility will be considered later in the chapter.

In my judgment, Montgomery County Council has, in the recent past, been influenced by the relatively high fiscal productivity of apartments in considering applications for rezoning. Certainly the successful rezoning lawyers who have handled many cases before the Council have consistently pushed this argument wherever possible. Citizens' groups—composed mainly of single-family house owners—in opposing apartment zoning have argued that apartments built in an area where the facilities were basically designed for single-family housing will produce congestion—of roads, schools, and recreational facilities. To some extent this may be an expression of their lack of faith in the public organizations charged with providing those facilities, and of their belief that the capacity of the facilities will not be increased in an appropriate way. Sometimes there are genuine problems in expanding capacity. For example, most schools are built when areas are originally settled, and the school sites are bought at a modest price, depending on how far in advance of requirements the school board purchases. But if the site has to be expanded in an already built-up area, it may be necessary to purchase sound existing houses and demolish them. The expansion of school facilities for the additional children brought to an area by apartment-zoning may be inexpensive if it has been planned in advance, but may become more expensive if it has to be provided at relatively short notice. The capacity of school buildings and grounds is one of the factors considered in each rezoning case, although it is not, and cannot be, an overriding consideration. The questions asked are usually related to present enrollments and capacity rather than capacity for the potential school population when the whole area is fully developed. There is not enough concern with the effect of rezoning on school planning.[18]

Precisely the same considerations hold if sewer mains have to be replaced with larger ones before the normal replacement date, or roads widened when this involves the demolition of buildings. Essentially, the difference is between the long-run cost, which can only be achieved for urban facilities when land use changes are planned far in advance, and the short-run cost of changing capacity within a limited time. The problem is very frequently exacerbated in growing areas because local governments pay a part of their capital costs out of current revenue—perhaps because of borrowing limitations. In Montgomery County, the council elected in 1962 pledged itself to reduce taxes and proceeded, rather freely, to rezone land for apartments and commercial uses. The objective may well have been to take advantage of the fiscal productivity of these uses in order to reduce tax rates for, and the amount of taxes paid by, the county's majority of single-family house owners. If so, they failed to distinguish between the short-run and long-run public costs of increasing the density of development, and they have not succeeded in reducing tax rates. In fact, in 1966 a county income tax was instituted for the first time.

The short-run costs of changing the density of development can be reduced somewhat if the changes are concentrated into a few areas so that, instead of having to enlarge many schools, sewers, playgrounds, and streets a little, a small number are enlarged a lot. Perhaps a new trunk sewer can be built to serve a large area of new apartments, an urban freeway built or extended to take care of its traffic, or a new school built. Apartments have become concentrated in some parts of the county but they have rarely been concentrated enough to take advantage of these kinds of economies, and it is not apparent that this has been a consideration in rezoning decisions.

Single-family house owners also oppose apartments for aesthetic and social reasons, as well as for reasons related to public expenditure and taxes. If the consensus of house owners is that living near apartments is undesirable for these reasons, house values near apartments will be

18. The problems of school planning are exemplified in a report of the Division of Planning, Department of School Facilities, Montgomery County Public Schools, *Report of a Study of Elementary School Needs with Total Land Development of the Colesville-Hillandale Area* (August 21, 1964). The report is based on existing zoning. However, it is forced to speculate on at least some potential rezoning decisions: "While we are not permitted to predict the future use of this land other than current zoning, its location makes it necessary to consider the possibility of its being rezoned. . . ." This clearly points out the conflict between using planning-zoning as a predictive and as a control device. In fact, there had been enough rezoning in the area within two years to seriously upset the plans developed in that report.

lower. Aesthetic and social preferences are part of the framework of economic decisions. Although planners and architects have generally applauded the variety of appearance which mixed densities of development give a residential area, there is no evidence that the typical suburbanite shares these views. Very possibly he is a suburbanite precisely because he appreciates trees more than buildings, no matter how attractive they may be, and especially more than high-density buildings. The social reasons for opposition to apartments are rather different. To some extent, house owners may object to living near apartments because they believe that *when* families live in apartments they behave in a less desirable way. Since they own no real estate they have less of a stake in the community. As they have no back yards of their own they make undue, and possible undesirable, use of public areas. But it seems more likely that house owners do not want to have living near them the *kinds of people* who live (or who they think live) in apartments. It is cheaper to live in some apartments than in houses and this may introduce a lower income group into the community. Apartment dwellers are almost certainly more mobile and for this reason are less "responsible" in some senses. But they may be more mobile because of their jobs rather than because they live in apartments. Some types of apartments may introduce many young people, though few apartment buildings with high proportions of efficiency and one-bedroom units are built in low-density areas because the young couples and single persons who occupy them prefer to be close to city, or at least suburban, centers. Later in the chapter the use of zoning for keeping undesirable land uses out of a local government area will be discussed. If the land use is generally considered undesirable for some reason, the jurisdiction which accepts it is disadvantaged. Often the poorest local government areas already have more than their share of such land uses, which are prevented from moving elsewhere. This affects the distribution of welfare between areas.

The particular features of land use that are chosen for zoning control can have a marked effect on land use patterns. For example, Montgomery County's residential density controls set maximum numbers of dwelling units per acre. The District of Columbia, on the other hand, restricts the floor space per acre. It is widely believed (though at least one unpublished study failed to support this) that small units rent for more per square foot of floor space. If this is true, Montgomery's ordinance, compared with the District's, encourages large apartment units. One implies that the undesirable external effects are related to the bulk of the building; the other, to the number of households. It is possible that conditions within the Washington SMSA vary so much that both ordinances are rational. But I suspect that the same conditions vary from site to site within a jurisdiction, and that both ordinances were drawn up without detailed examination of these points.

Co-ordination and Forecasting

The first function of planning is to influence land use decisions in the light of externalities; the second is to co-ordinate and forecast. Zoning is the main instrument available. In this section I will examine the reasons for, and the consequences of, its inadequacy in this respect. In order to make internally optimal land use decisions, it is necessary to project the future use of adjacent land and other land in the area. If the land use is expected to change, it is necessary to estimate when it will take place and, as precisely as possible, the nature of the change. One defect of zoning maps is that they contain no time dimension and therefore do not assist in estimating when a change in use will occur. Nor are they revised as frequently as they should be in order to reflect changing demands for particular land uses in particular areas. It is not clear whether these maps are supposed to provide a reliable forecast of future land uses or act as an instrument of control. Consequently, they fall between two stools and perform neither function adequately. They are most effective as an instrument of control when they are revised most frequently on the initiative of either planners or developers. But the more frequent the revisions (especially revisions which permit immediate change in use), the less effective are they for predicting future use.

In Montgomery County the forecasting–co-ordination function of zoning has recently been very largely superseded by private co-ordination of the type I discussed under the heading of land speculation (p. 109–13). It could almost be said that the most effective way to protect an area from apartment development would be for the planning commission to zone it for apartments. The price of the land would then rise beyond the cost, to the apartment developer, of buying land zoned for single-family housing and having it rezoned. Moreover, because the zoning can so readily be changed, many developers do not base their expectations on it when planning the use of adjacent land. Therefore, an apartment developer cannot, by buying apartment-zoned land, save anything on the costs of inducing desirable land use changes nearby. The costs of getting land rezoned—legal and managerial costs and interest and taxes on the land, or on an option on it—and the uncertainty as to whether rezoning will be granted, are simply an additional cost of development. They are generally less than the land price differential.

The existence of the zoning map may possibly increase, rather than reduce, uncertainty.

When a rezoning request is considered, the main emphasis by far is on the possible external effects. It is often difficult to argue that apartments will be an acceptable use for one plot of land and not for the plot next to it which is zoned for single-family houses. Effects on other land users may be much the same. But, if the forecasting and co-ordination function is taken seriously, the fact alone that for some time one plot has been zoned for apartments and the other has not is a reason for refusing to rezone. Other land users will have adjusted their uses in the expectation that the zoning map is a good forecast. The breakdown of the co-ordination function is cumulative. The more exceptions that are made, the less validity the zoning map has as a forecast; and the less validity it is known to have, the less reason there is to keep to it.

This failure is reflected in an argument made time and again by single-family house owners when opposing nearby apartment rezoning. They built or bought their homes in the expectation, based on the zoning map, that the area would remain a single-family housing area. Now they claim that these reasonable expectations are threatened. Of course, the forecasts that I have suggested would sometimes turn out to be wrong. Circumstances change and it is no more possible to forecast the future than it is to draw a zoning map that can be rigidly adhered to over long periods of time by even the most sensitive authority. But if the forecasts are recognized as such and are not linked to any developmental rights, and if compensation is payable, especially for unforeseen changes in nearby land use, the system should function more effectively.

Intrametropolitan Area Competition

Municipalities have, on occasions, used zoning as a means of frustrating the built-in income redistributional features of local public finance. Where incorporation has been relatively easy and municipal boundaries can be adjusted in the light of local political pressures, there has been plenty of scope for this kind of activity.[19] Large lot zoning has been one way that municipalities have been able to keep out poor families who, because of the way local government services are financed, would

19. For an interesting historical analysis of boundary changes within the Milwaukee metropolitan area, see Donald J. Curran, S.J., *The Financial Evolution of the Milwaukee Metropolitan Area* (Ph.D. thesis, University of Wisconsin, 1963). Curran explains many of the jurisdictional boundary changes on the basis of fiscal advantage. High-income residential areas and heavily industrialized areas incorporate to avoid having to contribute to the public costs—e.g., of education and welfare—for low income families.

have cost the public purse more than they contributed.[20] The courts have not permitted explicit discrimination on the basis of income, and have been hesitant about as close an approach to it as requiring houses of a certain size or value. But large lot zoning in an area where land prices are relatively high can have the desired effect and can be defended as necessary to safeguard health, safety, and public morals.[21]

Another famous example is the industrial enclave where industrialists avoid the redistribution of cost burden from industry to consumers which normally occurs through the property tax. In areas like Teterboro, New Jersey, where both the population and number of schoolchildren are very small, property taxes can be kept to a much lower level than in other parts of the state. This has been made possible by the incorporation of a municipality which has important functions and which is composed almost exclusively of an industrial area.[22]

It is not clear that these considerations have much significance for apartments in Montgomery County, Maryland. Firstly, because most of the local government functions in Maryland are performed by counties rather than by incorporated municipalities, there are very few municipalities in the state. County boundaries cannot be changed to provide tax havens. Then, again, apartments are neither as clearly profitable for the local fisc as industry, nor as clearly costly as low-income single-family houses. In fact, as I have already suggested, the County Council may have encouraged apartment developments partly because it believed them to be fiscally profitable, while single-family house owners may have opposed them, at least partly, because they believed them to be fiscally unprofitable. Most published studies would support the council's view. But experience seems to point in the opposite direction, partly because some capital expenditures are financed from current revenue and partly because the published studies generally assume that long-run adjustments to capacity can be made. But in part the published studies have not asked the right question. Even if they do return a fiscal profit, and assuming that apartment dwellers would otherwise have lived in the county in single-family houses, the building of apartments increases the burden on house dwellers. The families living in apartments would be more profitable to the county in homes. If, in the long run, they would

---

20. Bernard J. Frieden has looked at these problems in some detail. "Towards Equality of Urban Opportunity," *Journal of the American Institute of Planners,* Vol. 31 (1965), pp. 320–30.

21. Charles M. Haar discusses this in "Zoning for Minimum Standards," *Harvard Law Review,* Vol. 66 (1953), p. 1051ff., and in "Lionshead Lake Inc. v. Wayne Township," in *Land Use Planning* (Little, Brown and Co., 1959), pp. 235–44.

22. Morris Beck, *Property Taxation and Urban Land Use in Northeastern New Jersey,* Research Monograph No. 7 (Washington, Urban Land Institute, 1963). In 1960, Teterboro's population was twenty-two, including two schoolchildren.

otherwise have lived outside the county, the tax burden on house owners would be reduced. This argument neglects any possible effect of apartment living on the size of given families and on their need for welfare services.[23] One case in which fiscal consideration may have been important, because of the obvious advantages, was the rezoning of land for the Rossmoor Leisure World retirement community just outside the urban fringe in Montgomery County. Since all residents must be at least 52 years of age, this use of the land will generate no demand for schools. It is planned that the installment payments of residents will include health insurance and the developers will provide guards for safety and recreation facilities. But even here a total judgment depends on whether those involved would have lived in the county anyway, and whether, from a much broader point of view, a retirement community will contribute to the well-being of the county.

Part of the opposition of citizens' groups to apartment development may be based on the view that apartment dwellers are poor and will therefore become a burden to the community through welfare costs, or that they may include more criminals, delinquents, and broken families than would live in single-family houses. They object not only to the cost of welfare and police services, but also to the social diseconomies of having such people in the community. They also probably expect that Negroes will be able to rent apartments in the county more easily than they will be able to buy houses. In fact, many apartment managers have been as color conscious as real estate agents and house owners selling houses. Although these fears can be called by the apparently respectable name of social externalities, they can also be called discrimination. Whether they should be a factor in decisions about apartment development or not involves considerations of a much wider nature. Is it regarded as acceptable—in the interests of the metropolitan area as a whole—to segregate families according to any of these criteria? Given that local public finance does include some redistributive measures from richer to poorer families, from those without children to those with children, from the healthy to the sick, and from the fortunate to the unfortunate, is it acceptable to permit a sector of the population to opt out of their share of these expenses?

---

23. An interesting side issue is that the fiscal profitability of houses versus apartments has quite different implications for fully urbanized jurisdictions where new apartments replace houses, and for jurisdictions on the urban fringe where they can be additional to houses. In the latter case, even if apartment sites have to be cleared of houses, the present occupants are quite likely to locate elsewhere in the jurisdiction. In the fully urbanized area, apartment building seems more likely to change the population composition to one requiring fewer schools and different government services.

At present, Montgomery County has a high level of services with tax rates that are not high by national or Maryland standards. It is far from clear whether the increase in apartments in the county during the 1960's will, in the long run, serve to safeguard this situation or threaten it. Apartments appear to be changing the whole character of some areas and may, because most house owners do not like apartments nearby, lead to a depreciation in the value of the houses. The increase in the proportion of apartments in the total housing stock may lead to a higher proportion of families with children living in apartments. There is not much evidence of this as yet, although it is often claimed that older apartments house more children than newer ones. As competition from newer and more modern apartments increases, managements are prepared to relax their standards on numbers of children in the interests of keeping the apartments occupied. However, in a sample of 3,434 apartment units in Montgomery County, there were 717 public elementary schoolchildren in 1959 and in 1966 this had fallen to 600.[24]

Apartments may introduce some sections of the population which present residents would rather keep out because of race discrimination, because they might put an increasing load on welfare services, or possibly because they would bring some of the social problems at present concentrated in the District of Columbia to the county. The self-interest of county residents can best be served by keeping these problem families out. But, from a metropolitan viewpoint, is it better to have problem families concentrated in a "culture of poverty" in the central city, or to encourage them to disperse? Is it equitable that all the social and economic burden of their support should be placed on central city residents? Value judgments about who should pay for what, and have what privileges are involved in answering either of these questions but these judgments should give some weight to the values of the metropolitan population living outside the county.

Federal Government Taxes

So far we have been concerned with the effects of local governmental policies. It has long been believed that the federal government has encouraged house ownership as compared to renting by exempting the imputed rent of owner occupied houses from income tax. The owners of rented property have to pay income tax on their rent receipts but owners who live in their own houses are not taxed on the flow of

---

24. There is no record of numbers of junior- and senior-high school children at the earlier date. There were 318 in 1966 and this may be higher than in 1959. If a significant number of families stay in the same apartment for many years, the age distribution of the schoolchildren will change.

services which they receive themselves in lieu of rent. The encouragement which this gives to owning would not be as serious if the law was consistent in regarding housing as consumption. But some important items of expenditure on owner occupied houses are treated as if they were spent in the process of producing taxable income, and hence are deductable for tax purposes while, at the same time, the flow of services from the houses is treated as consumption and therefore not part of taxable income.[25] One effect has been encouragement of the development of co-operative apartments and condominiums for those who prefer living in multiple-family housing but want the tax advantages of home ownership. Significantly, this type of multiple-family housing has predominantly been high cost, appealing to those paying income tax at high marginal rates. However, most of the tax saving has gone to single-family house owners and has encouraged this type of housing.

Since 1954, the tax advantage has been at least partly offset by the accelerated rate at which investment in all income producing buildings, including apartments, could be depreciated for tax purposes. Chapter 2 outlines in some detail how this has worked, and how the concessional rate of tax on capital gains compared to other income has favored apartment over single-family house living. The object of accelerated depreciation is to encourage investment in buildings. In this chapter we are interested in whether the net effect has given more advantage to home owners or apartment owners. It is necessary to ask whether the special depreciation allowances and the capital gains tax concession to the apartment owner are, together, large enough to offset, or more than offset, the advantage of exemption from taxation of the imputed rent of the owner occupier. In principle, the capital gains tax concession is equally available to owners of rented and owner-occupied housing but, in practice, it is much less valuable to the owner occupant because of the inconvenience and the cost of the transaction when a single-family home is sold periodically in order to realize the capital gain. Further, the apartment developer can treat his profit in the construction process as a capital gain as long as he keeps the apartments for around seven to eleven years. This is impossible for the home builder because the administrative costs of renting are too high and the demand for new rented single-family houses may be quite limited. Again, the average

25. This question has a long history in the literature of public finance: e.g., Robert M. Haig, "The Concept of Income—Economic and Legal Aspects," in R. M. Haig (ed.), *The Federal Income Tax* (Columbia University Press, 1921); William Vickrey, *Agenda for Progressive Taxation* (Ronald Press, 1947), pp. 18–24; Richard Goode, "Imputed Rent of Owner Occupied Dwellings Under the Income Tax," *Journal of Finance*, Vol. 15 (1961), pp. 504–30.

house owner has a lower marginal income tax rate than the apartment owner. Whereas the house ownership concession is available on only one house to each person, the depreciation allowances and capital gains tax concession is available to any one taxpayer on an unlimited number of rented properties.

The value of tax concessions will vary with the marginal rate of tax being paid, and with other circumstances. Therefore, to get some indication of the relative magnitude of the two tax advantages, it is necessary to specify certain conditions and then ask how much lower the marginal tax rate of a house owner must be than that of an apartment owner before the value of concessions is equalized. Most of the assumed conditions are "conservative" in that the required difference in marginal tax rates is likely to be under- rather than overstated. This is shown in Table 17. All figures are expressed per $100 of investment in buildings under the following conditions.

Table 17. The Value of Tax Concessions to Apartment and House Owners

(Per cent of $100 building investment)

Type of ownership	Post 1964	1954–64
Apartment owner		
1. Cost = value for tax of building at completion	90.00%	90.00%
2. Depreciated value after 8 years at 5% on declining value	59.70	59.70
3. Present value of reduction in taxable income through accelerated depreciation	2.98	8.71
4. Taxable capital gains declared in year 8	10.00	22.29
5. Capital gains tax paid [(4) × 0.25 − discounted]	1.17	2.60
6. Compounded (at 7%) value of difference between cost and value at completion in year 8	17.07	17.07
7. Savings in taxable income from capital gains concessions [(6) + extra gains in (4)]	17.07	29.36
8. Present value of (7)	7.96	13.70
9. Present value of total reduction in taxable income [(3) + (8)]	10.94	22.41
House owner		
10. Annual reduction in taxable income	9.35	
11. Present value over eight years (a) 10 per cent discount rate	49.92	
(b) 20 per cent discount rate	35.90	

1. The opportunity cost of equity capital to the apartment owner is assumed to be 10 per cent. This is taken as his rate of discount and is the rate of cash return after loan repayment which is commonly "guaranteed" to syndicates that provide equity capital for apartment development. We assume that both the house and the apartment owner can

borrow the same fraction of the market value of the building at completion, on the same terms, so we can neglect the fact that the rate of return on equity capital is considerably greater than the over-all rate of return in our comparison. In real estate terms this factor is called "leverage." The house owner may have a higher discount rate since he is much more likely than the apartment owner is to be a "borrower," and on average the apartment owner probably pays a higher marginal income tax rate. In Table 18 the results are calculated, first, on the assumption that the rates of discount are the same and, second, on the assumption that the house owner's discount rate is twice that of the apartment owner. This range should include most cases.

Table 18. Marginal Tax Rates Required to Equalize Present Value of Concessions of Apartment Owners with Those of House Owners

House owner's marginal tax rate	House owner's discount rate (apartment owner's $=10\%$)			
	Post 1964		1954–64	
	10%	20%	10%	20%
14	74.6%[a]	56.6%	40.5%	29.2%
19	97.4[a]	73.0[a]	53.9	39.7
25	—	92.7[a]	67.3	51.7
36	—	—	91.8[a]	69.3

[a] Exceeds highest marginal rate of the federal income tax.

2. The apartment and the single-family house are both assumed to be owned for eight years and then sold. Since the change in value during that period is treated in the same way in both cases it can be ignored. It could be argued that apartments are more likely to increase in capital value, and are often sited with this objective. We will ignore this also. However, capital gains tax concessions are, of course, always more valuable to those paying taxes at higher rates. Also, the lower the discount rate is, the higher their present value. But this problem is separate from our main concern, and is not confined to residential or even to real property. The apartment developer-owner is assumed to construct his building for 90 per cent of market value at completion, and value it for depreciation at cost. The 11 per cent profit is treated as a capital gain when he sells the building.

3. The value of the capital gains concession on the profit made at the time of development is calculated by comparing it with what would have been paid if the capital gain had been compounded forward (as in line 6 of Table 17) at 7 per cent, and taxed as normal income when the

apartment was sold.[26] Most of the calculations assume that the rate of tax on capital gains is 25 per cent, which applies whenever the marginal tax rate equals or exceeds 50 per cent.

4. The normal rate of depreciation is 2 1/2 per cent per year but the apartment owner is assumed to make use of the law which permits double depreciation on the declining balance. By year 8 the advantages of this are becoming small; if he kept the building very much longer they would become negative. This is one reason for selling at somewhere around 7 to 11 years. Before 1964, he could treat the recovery of the extranormal depreciation on sale as a capital gain. The calculations are based on the assumption that the actual rate of depreciation of the building is not more than 2 1/2 per cent per year.

5. Land is assumed to be worth 10 per cent of the value of the buildings. In effect, the figures in Table 17 refer to $110 invested in land and buildings combined. This assumption tends to underestimate the relative level of concessions to house owners. Their concessions apply to both land and buildings while the apartment owner can only depreciate buildings, and land is generally a higher proportion of the total investment for the house owner than for the apartment owner. However, as discussed in earlier chapters, there may be more scope for the apartment owner to reap capital gains from increases in land values, even though land is a smaller proportion of the total value of apartment housing.

6. Net rent plus interest on the mortgage are assumed to be 7 per cent of the value of land plus buildings. Property taxes are levied at the national average rate of 1.5 per cent on the total market value. The tax concession to the single-family house owner in effect exempts gross imputed rent except for depreciation, repairs, and maintenance. The remaining three items are net rent, interest, and property taxes. The value of the concession is simply the present value of the tax that would have been paid on 8.5 per cent of the value of land and buildings, i.e., 9.35 per cent of the value of buildings alone, over the eight-year period.[27]

The technique adopted in Table 17 is to calculate first the present value of the reduction in the amount of income which is taxable at normal rates. This would equal the value of the concession if marginal rates were 100 per cent. As long as tax rates are assumed to remain

26. This is the alternative suggested by Joseph A. Pechman, *Federal Tax Policy* (Brookings Institution, 1966), pp. 90–93. It assumes that the gains can be identified and dated even when they are not realized on sale. A relatively low interest rate, like 7 per cent, would be necessary in order not to force owners with a high opportunity cost of capital to realize gains precipitately whenever they occur.

27. The small effect of depreciation on tax levels and any possible effect on imputed net rent are neglected.

constant over time, a given rate of tax on the present value is equal to the present value of the tax liability. Table 18 shows the rate of tax which an apartment owner would have to pay at the margin in order to get as much value from the concessions open to him as the house owner paying at the specified marginal rate would obtain. The rates in Table 18 are generally calculated by inserting the specified values for x (the marginal tax rate of the home owner) in the following equation,

$$(11)\ x = (9)\ y - (5),$$

where the numbers in parentheses refer to the values shown in different lines in Table 17, and solving for y, the required marginal tax rate of the apartment owner. If the resulting value of y was less than 50 per cent, the calculation of line (5) is invalidated and a different equation was used:

$$(11)\ x = (9)\ y - \text{discounted } (4)\ 1/2y.$$

Table 18 shows that, under present tax laws, if house and apartment owners have the same rate of discount, any house owner who pays income tax at all receives more benefit from the tax concession than any apartment owner. Even if the house owner has twice the discount rate, he must be paying tax at a very low marginal rate not to get more, even than the apartment owner who is paying at a very high rate. The situation was considerably more favorable to apartment developers between 1954 and 1964. But, even then, only house owners with a much lower tax rate and/or a much higher discount rate failed to do better.

My conclusion must be that the tax concessions available to single-family house owners give most of them greater advantages than are available to apartment owners. The over-all effect of the various tax concessions has been to encourage house over apartment building. Although the concessions available to apartment builders have received more publicity, they are not, and were not even at their height, large enough to affect the long-standing advantages to house owners of not having to pay tax on the imputed rent from their housing. However, concessions to apartment owners may make apartments somewhat cheaper and this may encourage some poor families to rent rather than buy, although many families paying low marginal rates could not afford to buy a house anyway. At the other end of the income scale, the accelerated depreciation provisions have encouraged some professional and business people with very high marginal tax rates to provide equity capital for apartment development.

The various concessions have no obvious effects on the location of apartments and single-family houses. Accelerated depreciation, and profits from development which can be treated as capital gains, are both greatest where the value of improvements is highest relative to land values; namely, in inner city areas.[28] On the other hand, the capital gains which accrue through increased land values are greatest where land values are changing most rapidly, particularly on the urban fringe. In these areas, too, there is most scope for the builder-speculator to influence the pattern of development in ways that will maximize the increase in the value of his land, as discussed in Chapter 6. In effect, he can, for example, turn part of his income into capital gain by hiring a good zoning lawyer. By contrast with both of these effects, the house owner's concessions are dependent mainly on the gross rental value of the house. However, they are of less value in areas where maintenance costs are high and houses are depreciating rather rapidly, as in the slums, because depreciation and repairs are not allowable as deductions. There is less encouragement to own old houses than new houses.

Income tax concessions have, on balance, favored house ownership rather than renting, though the difference was less marked during the 1954 to 1964 period. The 1964 change favored house ownership but the margin remains less marked than before 1954. Although these concessions have enabled the single-family house owner to bid more for land relative to the apartment developer, the suburban apartment developer who could arrange to take much of his profits in the form of capital gains, and could sell his apartments after getting most of the advantages from tax shelter, has still benefited considerably from these concessions. If his marginal tax rate has been high, he may have received as much benefit as some, especially the lower income families, among potential house owners. Competition among developers who had similar opportunities may have forced him to pass on part of the tax advantages in the form of lower rents or better facilities. If so, given the concessions to house owners, the effect of the concessions to apartment owners would be to persuade some families, otherwise at the margin between renting and buying, to rent.

Federal Credit

The federal government, through the Federal Housing Administration (FHA) and the Veterans' Administration (VA) mortgage provisions, has assisted house owners to borrow money for buying houses at lower

28. This provides an incentive for developers to overestimate the value of their buildings at the expense of land when they are claiming depreciation. It also makes the land under buildings an attractive investment for tax-exempt institutions, such as universities and churches, as shown by R. Bruce Ricks, in *Recent Trends in Institutional Real Estate Investment*, Research Report No. 23 (University of California, Berkeley, Center for Real Estate and Urban Economics, 1964), Chapter 4.

rates of interest than they would have been able to find in the free market. The FHA has also assisted apartment development, especially in urban renewal areas, in much the same way. In fact, the short-lived apartment boom of 1949–50 was due very largely to this type of financing. I have not investigated the provisions of the relevant legislation, nor its administration. There seems to be little doubt that for much of the postwar period federal provision of credit favored house owners. There is a need for careful investigation to find whether this bias remains and, if so, how strong it is.

Conclusions

There are no very obvious over-all conclusions to be drawn from examining the effects of these policies, adopted with different objectives by different levels of government. While federal credit and income tax provisions appear to favor the suburban home owner, local governments may, through zoning and taxing policies and through the pricing and investment policies of utilities, be favoring suburban apartment developers. There does seem to be a consistent bias in many of the policies examined which favors suburban fringe apartments over those in the central city, or even over those in suburban commercial centers. The costs of scattered urban development in terms of supplying public services have long been recognized, though their magnitude is a matter of debate. They apply to scattered apartment buildings as well as to scattered developments of single-family houses. Moreover, the apartment developer, because he can keep his apartments while they are appreciating, may be better able to reap gains from land speculation than can the tract home builder.

chapter 9

SUMMARY

A brief overview of the whole study and of significant findings are provided in this chapter. In the first section, the theory of short-run land use determination which emerges from the study is summed up. Because public policy is an important part of the institutional framework within which most urban land markets function, the rules under which this policy works have had to be taken into account in the theory. In the second section of the chapter, the reasons for the suburban apartment boom of the early 1960's are examined in the light of the theory. In the third section, suggestions are made about fruitful areas for research.

Private and Public Decisions in the Urban Land Market

It is almost impossible to imagine, in a city of any size, a land market which operates under a policy of pure laissez faire. At the very least, the public sector is likely to provide roads, water supply, and some form of waste disposal. In most cities, governments or government controlled utilities also provide public transport, telephones, and electricity. However, the government and its instrumentalities sometimes behave much as though they were competing private firms, and do not take advantage of their natural monopoly positions. Although there may be some difficulties, they should be able to set prices equal to long-run marginal costs and use benefit-cost investment criteria. This would enable them to bid for land against private users, and through such a market land could be allocated in an acceptable way.

In an unplanned land market, the operation of land speculators would be vital. Since land use decisions are indivisible in time, the best possible prediction must be made of the use of other land in the vicinity. Speculators specialize in making these projections and in owning land which may be subject to important and uncertain changes of value in the future. They can—and, in the interests of co-ordination, should—influence the use of other people's land in order to make their own more valuable. In fact, some of the best land use decisions may be made by speculators who own large areas of land and thereby internalize many of the use decisions that are external for the small owner.

However, these speculators are usually called "new town builders" or "planned neighborhood developers."

What should the public sector do in such a market? Private utilities have been in the thick of land speculation in much of the past urban development. Street car companies bought land for recreation at the end of their lines and railway companies bought the land alongside their tracks to sell to industrialists who would use the railway. But the public sector proper has been constrained by the lack of funds for investment, and by the efforts of private real estate interests to keep local governments out. Frequently, it has even been difficult for school boards to buy land in advance for schools and thus at least save the costs of appreciation.

But the land use decisions of a whole metropolitan area can be co-ordinated more effectively by the investments of governments and utilities than by the largest land speculator. Land use decisions in the public sector are so important in determining the direction and shape of metropolitan growth that they have always been a prime target for land speculators. Water supply, sewerage, roads, and schools probably contribute more to the value of land than almost any private land use in the vicinity. For the most part, opportunities have been missed because government bodies have not operated in a co-ordinated way and have often become the servants of real estate interests and because private utilities have not been controlled in this way at all.

There are two other interesting questions. If all the above services could be co-ordinated, would governments need to play any other role in the market through their planning-zoning powers? Or, if it is accepted that government and utility services will not be co-ordinated, can this function be performed through the use of the same powers? The first question can be answered yes, for two reasons. First, planning which includes expected private as well as public land use decisions can improve on planning which only includes the latter. Governments should assist in private land use projections because they are better equipped to do so than is any single private land user. They need to make projections of private uses in planning government services and these should be made public to all landowners and developers. This calls for an urban extension service something like the farm extension service.

Second, planning-zoning should influence individual land use changes whenever the whole community, or a group within the community, would be affected by a change in use. This should be done by governments, acting primarily for the whole community they represent and secondarily for groups within the community who do not have the power to act for themselves. It can influence land uses either positively or negatively, encouraging some in certain places and discouraging others.

The second question can be answered in much the same way, though land use planning which does not include the planning of public land use and utilities will probably be ineffective.

How do land speculation and planning-zoning interact? There appears to be a threshold of confidence in public planning which must be passed before it becomes effective. The public interest will begin to be reflected in projections when owners have to take it into account when they change land use. The more effectively the public interest is expressed, and the better the forecasts are, the more they will be accepted as one of the constraints on the private market. And, of course, the more they are accepted, the more effective they will become. An owner generally finds it in his interest to use land for a higher-density use than projected and to avoid compensating the community for injurious external effects. If he finds that others are not able to break through the constraints created by forecasts, he will accept them even though his returns may be a little lower. But if others are able to break them, he will be forced to try to do the same. Otherwise his competitors, through speculative gains, will be able to undercut his price for accommodation. Strong pressure to break the constraints does not necessarily imply that they are undesirable but only that they have not been accepted by many landowners. Of course, it is much easier to gain the confidence of private landowners in the integrity of the projections if they are used for public investment in land uses and utilities.

A local government may not be very good at acting in the interests of a group within its jurisdiction, but at least it is not likely to neglect the interests of the whole community. Within a metropolitan area the interests of local government areas can conflict, and the interests of the whole area need not coincide with the interests of individual jurisdictions. In general, the richer ones are able to come out on top in such conflicts. There is clearly a need for an authority at a metropolitan or state level which can act on behalf of the interests of the wider group.

The Suburban Apartment Boom

The general boom in the building of apartments in the United States is only partly explained by those characteristics of the urban land market which are assumed to increase residential density. In large SMSA's with high residential land prices and good public transport, apartments constituted a higher proportion of total housing stock built in the first half of the 1960's than they did in earlier years. The boom in apartments has been most marked, however, in cities in which this proportion was lowest in 1960. The strong causal forces, on the supply or demand side, seem to be geographically widespread. The most important of these is probably the recent increase in the proportion of the population in the age groups where apartments are most popular, and a long-run trend toward one- and two-person households. A more detailed examination of the changes in the family structure and age of apartment dwellers than has been possible in this study would be needed to pin down this influence.

The high proportion of apartments built in the suburbs during the 1960's is best understood as the latest phase in the general suburbanization of activities and the correspondingly slow rate of inner city redevelopment. These two trends have been considerably influenced by the way the land market works. Land use in most cities has been influenced more by speculation than by public planning. The speculator has found central cities to be relatively unfavorable. When the urban pattern is fairly stable, it is more difficult to assemble enough land to internalize externalities and to induce complementary use changes. The development of central areas is more often interesting to groups and whole communities than to single landowners.

Within the suburbs, the same differences occur between the well-established centers and the fringe areas where land use is changing much more actively. The latter gives the speculator much more opportunity to arrange and ensure the appreciation of his land. Suburban sprawl and scatteration appear to have been stimulated by the terms on which utility-type services are provided. They have tended to serve the interests of developers rather than of the whole community. They appear frequently to have been supplied at less than the full cost, covering the difference from charges which are not closely related to cost. This has especially encouraged scattered development on the urban fringe.

It is important not to lose sight of the changes in tastes which are, to a very large extent, behind the whole process of suburbanization. Increasing incomes and the flexibility afforded by the internal combustion engine have made suburban living an attractive and feasible alternative for the first time. However, it is not clear that the suburban apartment boom of the 1960's represents any significant change in tastes; if the whole boom could be explained by demographic changes, it does not. In fact, apartment dwellers are simply following house owners in demanding low-density living and the mobility which is possible in the suburbs. The important feature of apartments is not density; it is that they are rented. Even the high-rise apartments on the urban fringe are often built at quite low densities and appear to be largely a response to the premium some tenants are prepared to pay for height. Zoning decisions have sometimes been important too.

Property taxes of the type used in the United States discourage high-density development. These relatively heavy taxes on accommodation can only partly be passed on to the owners of capital. This is especially important when inner city areas generally have the highest property tax rates. The federal income tax structure also appears to favor house ownership over renting by exempting the imputed rent on owner-occupied dwellings.

In discussing the urban land market, it is impossible to avoid questions about equity and distribution of income. Inner areas are dominated by the relatively poor and the discriminated against. Because these people find it difficult to borrow, they are predominantly tenants, and tenants of old rather than new buildings. They cannot take advantage of the income tax concessions, but are affected by the property tax on their housing. One way to improve their position would be to lift at least part of the property tax from buildings and put it on land at a higher rate. By providing a perpetual mortgage at a uniform rate without requiring security, a land value tax permits poorer families to bid more effectively for land and become owners rather than renters.

The most potent forces in producing the suburban apartment boom have been on the demand side; demographic changes caused the boom and the long-standing desire for suburban living concentrated it in the suburbs. But had the land market operated more efficiently, there would probably have been less concentration in the suburbs, and within the suburbs there would have been less scattering of development around the fringe. Whole communities might be better if the location of the new apartments and the kinds of buildings which were permitted had been different.

Some Gaps That Should Be Closed

The theoretical arguments I have advanced require a great deal more empirical testing before they can be used with confidence. This is particularly true of the picture of the functioning of the urban land market. We know a good deal about how it works, but most of the literature is descriptive and lacks a theoretical framework—or it has a business framework which looks at real estate operations as individual decisions without paying much attention to their community implications. The assumption behind this monograph is that economic theory, and in particular welfare economics and public finance, provides a useful framework for looking at land use decisions.

We need to know much more about how the land development process works, and whether the model of land speculation presented here is useful. If the frictions in the market due to lack of knowledge, and non-economic reasons for holding land are so important that the economic model is unreal, we need to look for another, perhaps more behavioristic, model. How much land on the urban fringe is held for non-economic reasons? My feeling is that most landowners are very much affected by the possible selling price, the earning opportunities, and the rate of appreciation. Certainly historical factors, affecting, say, the size of lots, are very important. They can and should be considered in the model of speculation.

We also need to know more about the economic implications of zoning codes and the way they are administered. What do various parts of codes imply about the direction and magnitude of external effects of land uses? Are they administered in a way that permits them to perform both the projection and the influencing function satisfactorily? Are land speculators able to, and do they, influence both public and private decisions in ways that can produce an acceptable pattern of land use? Do different kinds of zoning codes, or even their presence or absence, produce any observable differences in patterns of land use between different jurisdictions?

The greatest gap in the data about the reasons for and the location of the apartment boom is: Who lives in apartments in different locations, at different densities and heights, and at different price levels? We need to know how age, family structure, and income distributions have changed since, say, 1960.

There would be high returns from a study of the apartment market which concentrated on building costs in different locations and at different standards and heights. These could then be compared with rents and vacancy rates. Is there a height premium for some kinds of apartments even on the urban fringe? How are rents and vacancy rates affected by age, the presence or absence of children, whether or not Negroes are admitted, provision of ancillary facilities, and location? Most of my work has treated location only in the grossest fashion and it deserves far more discriminating attention.

Designed by Edward D. King.

Composed in Optima text and Square Gothic display
by Monotype Composition Company, Inc.

Printed offset by The Murray Printing Company
on 60-lb. Perkins and Squier R.

Bound by The Murray Printing Company.